EN

WORKPLACE

USING SURVEYS TO SPARK CHANGE

Sarah R. Johnson

ATD Press is an internationally renowned source of insightful and practical information on
talent development, training, and professional development.

ATD Press
1640 King Street
Alexandria, VA 22314 USA
Ordering information: Books published by ATD Press can be purchased by visiting ATD's
website at www.td.org/books or by calling 800.628.2783 or 703.683.8100.

Library of Congress Control Number: 2018940842
ISBN-10: 1-56286-097-6
ISBN-13: 978-1-56286-097-4
e-ISBN: 978-1-56286-106-3

ATD Press Editorial Staff
Director: Kristine Luecker
Manager: Melissa Jones
Community of Practice Manager, Human Capital: Eliza Blanchard
Developmental Editor: Jack Harlow
Senior Associate Editor: Caroline Coppel
Text Design: Francelyn Fernandez
Cover Design: Alban Fischer, Alban Fischer Design

Printed by Color House Graphics, Grand Rapids, MI

CONTENTS

Foreword.. v

Introduction vii

Acknowledgments.. xv

Chapter 1: Engagement in the Workplace 1

Chapter 2: What Can a Survey Do?..15

Chapter 3: It Starts With Your Strategy 23

Chapter 4: Survey Strategy Drives Frequency 31

Chapter 5: Make Your Survey Dynamic.......................................45

Chapter 6: Getting to the "Why" of Organization Effectiveness........61

Chapter 7: Surveys Feed People Analytics 77

Chapter 8: A Consultant Mindset and Your Survey Strategy...........103

Chapter 9: Prepare Your Organization to Act.........................115

Chapter 10: Final Thoughts...125

References..131

About the Author..133

Index 135

FOREWORD

Sarah Johnson is a valued and respected member of the Perceptyx team, and I am honored to call her my friend, as well as my colleague.

With the candor that characterizes good friendships, Sarah reminded me recently that there was a time when I did not believe in consultants. My comeback was that my assessment was based on the fact that I had not met many good ones. In fact, Sarah is the one who changed my mind completely. She was my first encounter with a "real deal" consultant, so she became my guiding light.

As you read this book, you will see why Sarah is an effective consultant. She has deep professional experience, derived from insights learned through hundreds of client relationships over dozens of years. She has experienced the full spectrum of the survey business. Clients speak of her with almost reverent acclaim, and her colleagues know that if she is on the team, only good things will happen.

Yet, although Sarah is a professional, she is also practical. Instead of citing academic publications throughout this book, she refers to practical solutions, without mumbo jumbo or condescension. She is a survey expert, but she is eager to offer simple solutions, such as her 1-2-3 approach to survey action planning. In *Engaging the Workplace,* Sarah repeatedly calls for clearer definition of purpose and consistent communication, and provides suggestions that bias a survey toward success.

Employee surveys are extremely valuable. They provide an opportunity for a corporate conversation when employees want to be heard and management wants to listen. The timely insight gained from survey data in the hands of managers and HR professionals helps uncover the real issues in the workforce, so that strengths can be celebrated and problems can be solved. At Perceptyx, we enable people and organizations to thrive. Employee surveys help us to do that. That's why surveys remain our main purpose.

If you are a seasoned survey veteran, this book is the manual you wish you'd had 10 years ago. If you are just getting started with surveys, this book will give you a head start and a map to avoid the weeds. If you follow Sarah's advice, it may lead to the coveted "seat at the table" that HR professionals so desire, but are often denied.

Dave Belcher
Chairman, Perceptyx
July 2018

INTRODUCTION

Surveys have become an ubiquitous tool in organizations. Chances are the organization you work for conducts many surveys, whether it's to gather feedback on product and service satisfaction from customers or workplace engagement from employees. These internal surveys may focus on company processes and procedures, such as IT support or the food served in the company cafeteria. Employees may be asked to evaluate their manager in a 360-degree-feedback process. More than likely, the organization you work for conducts an employee survey designed to measure employee engagement on an annual or more frequent basis. These employee engagement surveys have become a standard event in most Fortune 500 companies, and many leading companies (think Google, Microsoft, and Amazon) have specialized staff dedicated to designing, administering, and analyzing employee survey data. Dozens of consulting firms, both large and small, provide survey administration and reporting services to organizations.

I fell into the business of organization surveys a bit by accident. My earliest professional position was an internship at IBM corporate headquarters in Armonk, New York. I worked in the personnel research department, which dates me a bit; the phrase *human resources* had yet to replace *personnel* in U.S. corporations. Our mission was to conduct research on strategic human resources issues and report our findings to leaders in the personnel (now human resources) function, as well as senior executives.

When I started my career at IBM in the 1980s, the company was considered a leader in the HR world. It hired professionals trained in human resources and industrial/organizational psychology before these fields of study had become commonplace in business schools, and when typical HR staffs were populated with individuals with company experience but no HR-specific training or expertise. IBM's HR function was well respected by its leaders and the general HR field, with its programs and practices considered leading edge.

IBM had implemented employee surveys as early as the 1950s, and was one of the first companies to regularly survey its employees. IBM was also one of the first companies to use surveys to measure not only the employees' experience with the company, but also a construct called employee "morale," a predecessor of employee engagement. Morale had a very specific meaning at IBM, and over the years the Morale Index became a critical number in the company. The regular company-wide surveys provided insight into long-term trends, differences in the experiences of different employee groups, and an important evaluation of leadership and leaders.

As the team that studied strategic human resources issues, the personnel research department also relied heavily on the methodology of employee surveys. Our work was separate from the ongoing morale surveys that another group within IBM's corporate human resources organization managed, and our focus was quite different. We looked at cultural differences across the organization. We used survey data combined with employee demographics to create predictive models of how many employees would participate in a voluntary early retirement program. We studied the link between IBM's Basic Beliefs and organization culture. We dove into employees' work-life balance issues. Our surveys of the executive population probed understanding and confidence in the business's strategy and operating efficiency. We evaluated compensation schemes and benefits programs based on employee feedback.

The data we collected from employees via surveys fueled a long list of critical studies that provided an ongoing stream of insight to IBM leaders. We were the team they called when faced with a decision that required insight about people and their behavior. Our work helped make the HR function in IBM truly a strategic partner to the company's leaders. The studies that we conducted were inspired by their information needs, and we routinely met with them to understand the topics that were of greatest value as they ran IBM's global business. Our work ebbed and flowed with trends in the company and in the business world. The studies we completed reflected what leaders needed to know at that time in the company's history.

Our research pivoted to meet business needs, and the early 1990s was a very difficult time for IBM. The company was in crisis. This was the beginning the personal computer's rise, and industry experts were predicting the death of the mainframe computer. IBM owned the mainframe market, which had traditionally generated an enormous amount of revenue and profit for the company, and had been slow getting into the personal computer market.

Industry analysts were describing IBM as bloated, slow moving, and obsolete, and were calling for the company to be broken into businesses to be sold off. Sales, revenues, and the stock price plummeted. John Akers, the CEO at the time, was forced out, and in a move that shocked employees, an outsider, Lou Gerstner, was brought in to run the company.

Any executive joining a company as CEO wants and needs to understand the situation they are walking into. So shortly after Gerstner joined IBM as the CEO and chairman of the board, our team surveyed the company's top executives on strategy, execution, and culture-change issues. The survey's purpose was to assess the current landscape and what was on the mind of Gerstner's top lieutenants, the team responsible for leading the company in a new direction.

As one part of the project, my team and I ran an analysis that produced a profile of the executive team, reflecting their willingness to change with the times and participate fully in the transformation of IBM. The analysis allowed us to estimate how many leaders were ready to lead, how many needed more convincing, and how many were digging in their heels and resisting change. The analysis provided powerful and sobering insights into the challenges ahead.

Not long after this work was completed and shared with senior leadership, I was reading an interview of Gerstner published in *USA Today*. He was asked what challenges lay ahead. He replied, "We recently did an analysis that helped me recognize that there are a number of senior leaders who aren't ready for change." I couldn't believe it! He was mentioning my analysis and insights. The analysis my team had completed had shaped the CEO's perception of the task ahead of him, and influenced his plan of attack. I realized then how survey results, when focused on the right topics and analyzed to provide true insight, could influence the thinking and actions of senior executives.

More Than Check the Box

My experience in personnel research at IBM opened my eyes to the power of employee surveys and the strategic value they can provide organizations. And while I carried that experience and focus to other organizations I have worked for as an internal or external consultant, I found that in many cases the company's survey had become a "check the box" experience or an exercise in collecting data that were used very narrowly. Too many organizations utilize surveys with a limited focus (to simply measure engagement, as an example) and collect little data that help illuminate critical issues. Other companies ask just a handful of survey questions that provide metrics, but not much in the way of deep understanding of organizational issues.

These types of surveys are a lost opportunity to not only drive organization effectiveness, but also establish HR as a strategic partner to the organization's leaders.

The human resources function has long aspired to have a seat at the table with leaders of the company, and has recently realized that data and analytics are a critical tool to make this happen. Senior leaders live in the world of numbers and are fluent in its language. HR functions must develop the same capability. Data and analytics have the ability to transform the HR function into a source of data-based guidance. Analytics can provide insight into culture, leadership, organization change, attrition, customer focus, mergers and acquisitions, employee development, globalization—and employee engagement.

And at the heart of data and analytics is the organization survey, the most strategic and influential program the HR department can implement. A survey touches every employee in the company at the same time, sending a message about what is most important to the company at that moment. Survey results and insights are provided to all divisions, business units, and locations. With access to survey results for their team, managers will be asked to participate in a process of interpreting and acting on the results. Senior executives will be debriefed on the overall findings. These leaders will then discuss the results with managers and employees via emails, videos, and town hall meetings. The results might even be shared with the board of directors. What other HR program or practice has that much reach, that much influence, across the organization?

Untapped Potential

While the majority of organizations conduct some sort of employee survey, many miss the opportunity to collect strategic information or mine the data to provide the insights necessary to drive organization effectiveness. Few HR functions use the survey process and results to become a strategic partner to senior executives. And here's what is most frustrating: It's not difficult to transform an employee survey into the engine for an HR analytics strategy that truly drives the success of the organization.

When designed, executed, and analyzed properly, organization surveys enable leaders to made data-based decisions about people. Survey results can provide important guidance for the implementation of the organization's strategy. Surveys can assess the success or failure of organization initiatives such as leadership development, performance management, beliefs and values, diversity and inclusion, communication of organization direction, and even mergers and acquisitions. Surveys can collect insights into what programs, practices, or management capabilities are most valuable to employees and help retain key talent. The results can enable HR staff to provide programs and guidance based on data, rather than on fads, trends, or guesses about what is needed. The staff that controls the data can wield much influence in the organization, and become key advisers to leaders across the business.

This book will help you make the most of a process and tool that likely already exists in your company. It will help you design a process that collects employees' views on critical issues, wring as much insight out of the data as possible, and drive organization performance. Let the employee survey make you a valuable strategic adviser to senior leaders in your company.

What's in This Book

Here's a brief overview of the chapters:

Chapter 1, "Engagement in the Workplace," lays the groundwork for the shift in organizations from surveying employees about satisfaction with the company to surveying to assess their level of engagement. However, the chapter notes that when the organization's survey focuses exclusively on engagement, it is wasting a valuable opportunity to learn about what makes the organization effective. Assess and enhance the workforce environment, and engagement will come along for the ride.

Chapter 2, "What Can a Survey Do?" challenges the idea that just by having a survey, the organization will fix all its problems. Asking questions and collecting data won't drive change. What happens after the survey is far more important.

Chapter 3, "It Starts With Your Strategy," asks the question that needs to be answered before moving on to survey design: Why conduct a survey in the first place? Survey programs that provide insight into critical company strategies and direction will drive change and enhance the value of the survey program.

Chapter 4, "Survey Strategy Drives Frequency," addresses the common misconception that acquiring more data more frequently trumps all other strategies. In fact, the organization's survey strategy should drive survey frequency, not the other way around. More data do not necessarily translate into more action. Build the right survey design and frequency to fuel the analytics engine.

Chapter 5, "Make Your Survey Dynamic," makes the case for bucking the "one size fits all" trend in survey design. After all, your company is not like any other company. Design a survey that matches your company's unique issues and information needs. Plus, what's important to your company can change over time. Balance following historic trends with refreshing the focus of the survey.

Chapter 6, "Getting to the 'Why' of Organization Effectiveness," argues that while measuring engagement is important, the organization is better served by understanding the reasons behind it. Understanding the workplace factors that influence engagement and success will lead managers to the right actions.

Chapter 7, "Surveys Feed People Analytics," shows how relying on your gut could undermine your credibility with leaders in your organization. Actions based on beliefs and assumptions, or implemented in the wrong place in the organization, use up resources and do little to influence critical issues. Use analytics to identify the right actions.

Chapter 8, "A Consultant Mindset and Your Survey Strategy," delves into the role change that HR professionals need to embrace to best serve their organization. HR business partners can play a critical role as engagement consultants to senior leaders.

Chapter 9, "Prepare Your Organization to Act," makes taking action as simple as 1-2-3. While the organization might be inclined to ask the world of managers to justify the amount of time spent on designing and administering the survey, an overly complex process is the enemy of getting managers to act. Make action planning simple and foolproof.

Chapter 10, "Final Thoughts," ties it all together. What does your organization need to know, and what does it need to do, to become effective and achieve its goals? HR professionals who can answer that question and provide the data and insights leaders need will lead the pack to create an engaging workplace.

This book is intended for HR practitioners, not academics or researchers. That's not to say that research findings aren't important to the practice of surveys and employee engagement. They absolutely are. But the intent of this book, first and foremost, is to provide simple, practical, and easy to implement ideas and solutions to get the greatest value out of your organization's survey.

ACKNOWLEDGMENTS

The majority of graduate programs in industrial/organizational psychology don't offer classes in employee engagement and organization surveys. Those of us who have spent our careers consulting in this field have gained our knowledge primarily through experience, sharing best practices, and learning from one another.

At its core, consulting is all about teaching clients, expanding their knowledge and insights. The knowledge I have gained, the expertise I have acquired, and the philosophy I teach to my clients is the product of the many wonderful professionals who have taught me.

My thanks to Allen Kraut, who gave me my start in surveys first as a graduate-student intern and then as an associate at IBM. Allen has been a generous and insightful mentor, collaborator, and colleague for more than 30 years.

My husband, Bill Johnson, has been my survey research partner for many years. Bill is the most creative statistician I have known in my career, and his innovative approach to survey analytics has both delighted clients and shaped the thinking of many consultants over the years. No one can make data sing the way Bill Johnson can. Many, many thanks for the inspiration and support you have unselfishly provided over the years.

The survey research teams I led at IBM, Eastman Kodak, Genesee Survey Services, and CEB provided an endless supply of ideas and insights, and working together we pushed the practice and science of organizational surveys into new territory.

The time I have spent at Perceptyx has been the cherry on the top of my career in organizational survey consulting. Dave Belcher, Jack Morehouse, and John Borland have given me the professional freedom to spend my time on the aspects of consulting that give me the greatest joy. Jack's groundbreaking research and thinking on engagement and survey practices is at the core of the Perceptyx philosophy, and is reflected in much of what you will read in this book. Thank you from the bottom of my heart for allowing me to be part of your organization.

Most of all, endless thanks to Fran and John Rassenfoss, who made everything possible.

Sarah Rassenfoss Johnson
July 2018

1

ENGAGEMENT IN THE WORKPLACE

Organizational surveys have always been about something. Whether it was job satisfaction, morale, or commitment, surveys have always had a focal purpose and metric. This focus area is the survey's reason for being, why it was being done in the first place.

Organizations have been using surveys as early as the 1940s; they became increasingly more common in the 1950s, 60s, and 70s, achieving commonplace status in the 1980s and beyond. Today, the majority of organizations conduct some sort of employee survey. A recent study found that 76 percent of Fortune 500 companies survey their employees annually, and 61 percent of midsized companies conduct an employee survey at least once per year (Masztal et al. 2015).

Early examples of surveys focused on the workplace and job satisfaction, and included questions about job elements, co-workers, and management, as well as relatively mundane topics like the cafeteria and parking lot. Over time, survey content evolved to include questions about the company, confidence in leadership, and satisfaction with pay, benefits, and job opportunities. Job satisfaction as a focal area evolved into organization satisfaction. Many companies developed unique content that reflected their employment philosophies, such as the IBM Morale Index, which I worked with early in my career. Academics created and validated scales measuring satisfaction, which could be included in their research on job or organization satisfaction, as well as in an organization's survey.

Much research had been conducted over the years to demonstrate the value of surveys in organizations and the importance of metrics such as job or organization satisfaction. This research sought to connect job and organization satisfaction with important business metrics such as stock performance, sales, profits, and turnover to demonstrate the monetary value of investing in employees and building strong employee relations.

While the research found statistical relationships between the measures, the direction or causality of this relationship varied from study to study. In some studies, job or organization satisfaction was a driver of organization performance metrics. In others, organization performance metrics were drivers of job or organization satisfaction. The logic behind satisfaction driving organization performance made sense, as did the logic of organization performance influencing employee satisfaction.

So which was it? What should organizations do to maximize success? Should they improve employee satisfaction to enhance organization performance, or was it more important to enhance organization performance to grow employee satisfaction? Clearly both satisfaction and performance were important, but the equivocality of their relationship caused some organization leaders to question the quality of research and the value that employee satisfaction and surveys brought to the organization. If the relationship wasn't clear or consistent, wasn't it simply a waste of time and money to conduct an employee survey and act on the results?

From Satisfaction to Engagement

Beginning in the late 1990s, a new focus area for surveys emerged: employee engagement. While employee engagement shared many of the same characteristics as job and organization satisfaction, it differed in a fundamental way. Satisfaction as it was originally conceived focused on how employees felt about the organization. It measured the extent that employees' expectations or needs were fulfilled by the organization or the job. Did the organization deliver what was implied or promised? Employee engagement included this element of satisfaction (although it didn't use the word *satisfaction*), but went further to incorporate how employees behaved or intended to behave based on whether their expectations or needs were met. The behavioral elements of engagement included:

- **Discretionary effort:** How hard were employees willing to work for the organization? Would they go above and beyond for the company?
- **Intention to stay with the company:** How likely were employees to look for another job?
- **Advocacy behavior:** Would employees be willing to recommend the company as a good place to work, or would they recommend the company's products or services to others?

The addition of a behavioral element clarified the relationship with organization performance metrics. Employee engagement as a metric made sense to senior leaders. Engagement wasn't just about "feelings," those squishy things that some senior leaders didn't know what to do with. It was also about important actions: Were employees willing to give the company their all, and was the company able to hold on to top talent? These questions are important enough on their own, but even more so given the relationship between engagement and organization performance. Study after study found that employee engagement had a direct and positive influence on turnover, sales, profits, inventory turns, customer satisfaction, and more. On his website, author Kevin Kruse (2012) maintains a compendium of research studies linking employee engagement to multiple business outcomes.

Employee engagement took off like wildfire. As an external consultant, I was astonished at the wave of companies and leaders that wanted to talk about engagement, learn about it, implement a first-ever survey focusing on engagement, or retool an existing organization survey to focus on engagement. Senior leaders spoke to their employees about engagement in town hall meetings. Others were quoted in articles about how important engagement was to the success of their organization. Engagement became widely understood and accepted by leaders in a way that job and organization satisfaction never did. So great was the influence of engagement on the vernacular of senior executives around the globe that a Deloitte study found that 87 percent of organizational leaders view engagement as one of their top challenges (Brown et al. 2015). The rate of engagement's adoption as an important metric for organizations and the degree to which leaders embraced it was extraordinary.

Early research on engagement identified its basic building blocks of commitment, discretionary effort, intention to stay, and advocacy behavior, although there was a fair amount of variability between the researchers studying the topic. Some included questions measuring absorption in tasks or the job, or the perceived speed with which the workday went by. Consulting firms that worked with client organizations to design and administer surveys added their spin to the metric, including elements such as enablement or the organization context. Organizations themselves further modified the construct to reflect their culture and focus.

Before long, employee engagement became a fractured construct. A Google image search of the phrase *employee engagement models* will return pages and pages of divergent approaches to conceptualizing and measuring employee engagement. The plethora of models has created confusion for leaders and HR professionals. Which is the best? The most accurate? For the most part, they share common elements, and each has benefits and failings. And to be honest, many of them work in the right context.

Even more concerning was the fact that employee engagement had become an obsession. Many senior leaders focused on their employee engagement "score"—that is, the average percent favorable score for all questions in the engagement category—and its change from previous surveys almost to the exclusion of every other metric in the survey. Managers were stack-ranked on their teams' employee engagement score, with the bottom-scoring managers required to participate in special development programs, subject to additional coaching, or even pulled from a management role. Engagement scores became a factor in making decisions on promotion or leadership potential. One CEO announced that his goal was for the company to have the highest engagement scores in the industry. As managers and leaders felt the pressure to maximize employee engagement scores, it is no surprise that some of them turned to more nefarious plans, including pressuring employees to respond to the survey questions favorably.

As would be expected, plans were developed across organizations to improve employee engagement. After all, feedback and action planning are two of the cornerstone activities of the survey process. But given the obsessive focus on engagement in some organizations, managers and leaders occasionally turned to simple feel-good actions, such doughnuts, pizza, and employee appreciation parties, to boost engagement. Actions became increasingly shallow in many organizations, encouraged by a new industry of suppliers of employee recognition products and events said to drive engagement. Just about everything was identified as an influencer of engagement, from vacation time to T-shirts to plaques to wearable fitness devices.

When the Focus on Engagement Is Too Much

Some of you might have read the preceding paragraphs and thought, "So what's the problem here?" What could be wrong with having leaders who are focused on employee engagement, particularly if it drives company performance? Shouldn't managers get counseling if their teams have low engagement scores? And doesn't it make sense that the worst offenders should be moved out of management? How is it wrong to treat employees to doughnuts or pizza or parties?

On the surface, nothing. Employee engagement is a very important construct in organizations. The impression that it has made on senior executives' thinking is extraordinary. There is no denying that the link to business performance has been essential in making employee engagement a critical focus area in companies around the world, resulting in the implementation of valuable actions in many organizations. Many leaders have been enlightened to the value that employees bring to their organizations, and the payoff that can be gained by investing in employees.

But at the same time, leaders may not know what to do about it. The Conference Board reported that while 90 percent of executives understood the importance of employee engagement, less than half understood how to address the issue (Ray et al. 2014). Without a complete understanding of the issue, it is no surprise that leaders gravitate to what they do best: Focus on the numbers and metrics.

As a result, many leaders and HR teams have a narrow understanding of employee engagement and how to address it in their organizations. Generally, employee engagement is one of many measures in an organization survey. A well-constructed survey measures employee engagement in addition to other important elements of organization effectiveness, ranging from the job itself, to relationships with managers and leaders, to opportunities for development and career growth, to compensation and benefits. These elements help diagnose organization health and indicate productive areas for action and improvement. Many of the elements are themselves drivers of engagement, meaning they can increase or decrease employee engagement depending on how effectively they are implemented in the organization.

Some organizations have become so focused on the employee engagement score—the number produced by the survey—that they have forgotten the point of the survey. Too many well-written and comprehensive surveys end up being boiled down to a single metric or number that leaders dwell upon.

I can understand how this happens. HR functions have long striven to be strategic partners with the C-suite. Being a strategic partner often requires coming to the table with data, and surveys can provide no end of data. And the link between the employee engagement score from the survey and organization performance metrics was a boon to many HR functions.

However, what started out as a great opportunity to connect with leaders and influence their thinking about the role of people in the company has instead produced a limited focus indeed. I have worked with multiple clients who collected survey data on many topics, but only shared the engagement scores with their leaders, cut by demographics such as business unit, country, tenure, or job type. Despite arguments to provide an analysis of all survey results, they resisted, not wanting leaders to lose their focus. In some cases, even if they did present a broader interpretation on the overall health of the company, the only data leaders were interested in were the engagement scores. Employee engagement has become the hook of the survey.

Such narrow focus is a lost opportunity, for many reasons. First and foremost, employee engagement is an outcome measure. This means that employee engagement cannot be influenced directly ("Be more engaged!!") but rather through elements of the work experience that have been shown to affect employee engagement. These elements vary from company to company in terms of their influence on engagement, but often include the work employees do, their ability to be successful in the company, empowerment, confidence in the future of the organization, the capabilities of colleagues, communications, opportunities for career growth, and their relationship with managers. These elements are as important to measure and understand as employee engagement. They all influence organization success in their own way, and each deserves study, interpretation, and action for the organization to be effective. However, they have often been undervalued, as employee engagement has become overvalued.

This is not in any way to say that employee engagement is not important. It absolutely is, and it deserves attention. But when we allow it to become the primary focus of the survey results, then we have done the organization a disservice. We have prevented the organization from accessing important information that can enhance its overall success.

Beyond Employee Engagement

The focus of the organization survey shouldn't be employee engagement, but organization effectiveness. Engagement is one of many elements that make up organization effectiveness. Rather than focusing on *employee engagement* as a noun—a score, a thing, or a target to be achieved—we should focus on *engage* as a verb. How can we engage employees? What can we do to create an organization and a work environment that is engaging for employees? Employee engagement was never meant to be about the score, but what the survey results can tell the organization about how successfully it is engaging employees in its mission, strategy, and objective. Achieving high levels of employee engagement is the end product of creating a work environment that is engaging. It is time to think differently about what employee engagement is, and the role it plays in organization effectiveness and in organization surveys.

Every organization aspires to be successful, although success can be defined differently across organizations: dominant market share, high profits, strong year-over-year growth, the highest customer satisfaction, or the most innovative products. Each has a strategy and set of objectives, inspired by its definition of and criteria for success. An organization's success is influenced by performance, both individual and organizational. It requires clear focus and direction, ample access to resources, the right talent with the right skills, and efficient processes designed to deliver on the company's objectives. Performance is also a function of employee engagement, as we have learned through years of research. Employee engagement influences performance, which in turn influences organization success. This relationship is pictured in Figure 1-1.

What we sometimes forget is that organization success can have a significant influence on engagement. All of us can think of examples of successful companies with high engagement, and unsuccessful companies with understandably low levels of employee engagement. That makes sense. But in reality, it is more nuanced than that: There are successful companies with low levels of employee engagement and unsuccessful companies with high levels of employee engagement. So what gives?

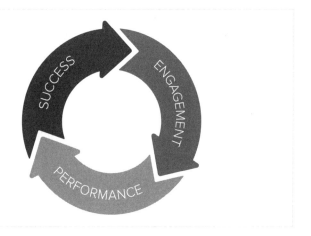

Figure 1-1. Relationship Between Success, Engagement, and Performance

A few years ago, I was speaking about this topic at a conference when an HR business partner at a local company approached me. She described a fast-growing, dynamic company that had recently had an exponential increase in sales and profitability, and was hiring large numbers of new staff daily. The company was getting great press, and the sky was the limit for its growth. But she told me that its employee engagement scores were very low, which was a bit of a mystery to senior leaders. She wondered why employees were so unhappy in the midst of such success.

As we talked more, a few things became apparent. Employees were working ridiculous hours. They rarely had the tools and resources required to accomplish what was being asked of them; the workplace philosophy was to get the work done no matter what. They were developing processes and procedures on the fly as the company expanded, and the way work was to be completed was continuously evolving. Performance goals and objectives were as ill-defined as work processes and procedures, so employees were concerned that their accomplishments would not be adequately evaluated on performance reviews, or recognized through salary increases, bonuses, or even compliments. Employees didn't see a path forward for their skill development or career growth. They were overwhelmed and felt as though the organization's success was solely the product of their blood, sweat, and tears. The HR partner said that if you walked through the office, it was clear that there was no joy, excitement, collaboration, or fun—and no hope that things would get any better.

The company was successful, but its employees were not. Organization success does not always translate into high levels of employee engagement. I have worked with several organizations that were highly successful but had low levels of employee engagement. The common denominator in each of these companies was the employees' inability to anticipate and achieve their desired level of success in the company. Employees reported that they were working day and night, often with substandard tools and resources and with inefficient processes. The companies were successful, but that success required a herculean effort on the part of employees. Burnout rates were high, and opportunities for development and career growth were limited or nonexistent. Employees did not see a future for themselves; they stayed only long enough to add the experience to their resumes.

Most of these companies emphasized the success of the organization at all costs. The success of employees either wasn't considered important, or the company failed to invest the time and resources necessary to help employees recognize their opportunities to be successful. These were not companies that built loyalty or camaraderic, and they certainly struggled to retain their best employees.

It's not enough for the organization to be successful to influence employee engagement. Employees need to feel confident they can be successful in the organization. They need to be able to anticipate their success as a member of the organization. Just as different organizations have different definitions of success, each employee can have their definition of personal career success in that organization. The goal for organizations is to provide a work environment where employees can succeed not only in their role as a contributor to the organization's goals and objectives, but also personally through doing rewarding work, interacting with talented and collaborative colleagues, being recognized for their contributions, and growing in the company in a meaningful manner.

When organizations place too much emphasis on an employee engagement score, they fail to understand the broader picture of what it is like to work in the company. They sacrifice the opportunity to understand if they are providing the right work environment to attract and retain critical talent. They won't uncover the obstacles to effective processes and communications. They won't learn what employees need to understand to have confidence in the organization's future. They have lost a critical opportunity to overcome barriers to achieving success.

Where the Survey Fits In

Survey content, to be truly effective in driving organization success, must be multifaceted. A comprehensive survey will do more than just measure employee engagement; it will evaluate organization effectiveness, identify barriers to effective performance, and provide the data necessary to understand the factors that influence both engagement and employees' anticipation of their success in the organization. The survey can pinpoint where decision making is stalled, communications are breaking down, and work processes are slow. It can indicate where additional training is required, where resources are constrained, and where culture is discouraging employees from taking the risks required to create innovative products and services.

It's not just about engagement. It's about effectiveness and success, both at the employee and organization level.

The good news is that as attracted as senior leaders are to employee engagement, they are more interested in identifying and overcoming obstacles to effectiveness. Identifying ways to improve organization performance is music to their ears. Expanding the focus of the survey beyond employee engagement provides rich data that can be used in many ways and across many functions and subunits within the organization. It transforms the survey from being a tool with a single-metric focus into one for diagnosis, change, and improvement.

Here are six steps to broaden the focus of your organization's survey:

1. Reframe the purpose of the survey. Rethink the survey's name and branding to focus on organization effectiveness and link it to important organization initiatives such as strategy and objectives.

2. Spend time with senior leaders, both to capture the data and insights they need to run the business and to shape their thinking on what the survey can do for them strategically. Share examples of how survey data analytics can provide critical insights that drive important change.

3. Create a communications strategy that places employee engagement in the context of organization effectiveness, signaling to the organization that the survey is about more than just generating an employee engagement score.

4. Sharpen the content of the survey to include questions that address the fundamentals of organization effectiveness. Write questions that are actionable at multiple levels of the organization, from the most senior leaders to frontline managers and supervisors.

5. Present a comprehensive review of the survey results to leaders. Share engagement scores, of course, but spend

more time discussing the barriers to effectiveness—and, consequently, the barriers to high levels of employee engagement.

6. Refocus action planning from improving employee engagement scores to removing the barriers to performance and enabling employees to anticipate their desired success in the company. When organizations focus on enhancing performance and success, employee engagement comes along for the ride.

The popularity of employee engagement among senior leaders has been very effective in creating interest in and commitment to surveying employees. That's great news. Now that we have their interest, it is time to shift their focus from just employee engagement to a more comprehensive and strategic use of organizational surveys and data in the company.

2

WHAT CAN A
SURVEY DO?

At its most basic, a survey is a tool to collect data, a method for gathering information and conducting research. There are many ways to collect employee insights, such as interviews, focus groups, internal and external social media channels, and even suggestion boxes. While all these are useful, they don't scale well in large organizations, and are not a practical approach to collecting input from a broad and representative group of employees.

Surveys, on the other hand, provide an efficient means for asking questions and collecting answers, and they are well suited for amassing a lot of data from a lot of people. Surveys are highly scalable, and the methodology works well in both small, local companies and multinational corporations with tens of thousands of employees. And yet, while surveys are a means of collecting insights, somehow there is an expectation that surveys can transform organizations.

I have heard clients say, "Our surveys haven't changed anything in this company." Well of course they haven't. Their mistake was to expect the surveys, on their own, to change anything. The sole purpose of a survey is to collect input from employees. The survey itself won't fix anything, and if it's not properly worded and structured, it may not even tell leaders what they really need to know. So, the important question leaders need to ask themselves is what can a survey do?

Surveys Start a Conversation

Consider for a moment a typical conversation you might have with someone. The conversation might be short and breezy or long and in depth. It might focus on the weather or recent controversial events. It could be one sided, with one participant doing most of the talking, or it might be a lively back-and-forth, full of insights and suggestions.

At its essence, a survey is nothing more than a conversation, scaled up between hundreds, thousands, or hundreds of thousands of employees. It is an efficient approach to asking questions and collecting answers. And just like any other conversation, a survey can be breezy or in depth, one sided or fully engaging both parties. The quality of the conversation reflects the interests of the parties, the participants' level of comfort and trust, and the company's willingness to ask difficult questions, listen to what could be uncomfortable responses, and then do something about it.

Conversations that involve asking questions and simply listening to the answers can be great. One party shares their perspective and gets a few things off their chest, while the other gains new insights. That, in a nutshell, is all that a survey really does: asks questions, collects answers, and shares them with the people in the organization who need to listen.

But imagine a conversation where one side asks questions that don't make sense, or asks about the weather when the other side really wants to talk about how their day has been. Some questions might be on unfamiliar topics, making them unclear and difficult to answer. Think about how you would feel if you were stuck in that type of conversation. You might be frustrated, bored, even annoyed. You might think the other person is clueless about what is important or relevant to you, and you would likely want to end the conversation as quickly as possible and avoid speaking with them in the future.

The conversation that the survey represents needs to ask the right questions and listen to the responses with an open mind. But if it stops there, nothing is really gained. It's possible a few managers and leaders, after reviewing the responses, might be inspired to rethink their beliefs and assumptions, and some may even change how they behave at work or how their part of the organization operates. But without any imperative to share results, guidance on how to act, or clear expectations for how survey data should be used, managers typically do little. If this pattern continues survey after survey, most organizations will see their survey participation or response rate steadily decline. Why?

Well, from the employee perspective, what's the point in participating? They shared their views, they expressed their opinions, and management listened. Great, but at some point employees want to see things change. They want their answers to the survey questions to make the organization different, and to make their experience in the organization different. Year after year of answering followed by no change or improvement rightly seems pointless.

Organizations that repeatedly run surveys without acting may find that their survey program produces the opposite of the desired effect. Instead of improving engagement or trust in the organization, employees are less engaged and less willing to trust senior leaders. Giving employees the opportunity to speak up can raise their hopes that their opinion matters and that things will change. When that doesn't happen, cynicism grows and trust is broken.

Surveys Are a Means to an End

A survey is just one step in a much longer process of listening, discussing, and acting. A critical element, to be sure, but on its own it doesn't lead to insight or action. The survey must be embedded in a multiphase process that includes strategy development, content development, analysis, feedback, action planning, and most important, action taking—because just planning the actions creates activity, but not much improvement.

But most organizations spend the bulk of their time and attention on the survey, to the exclusion of the other equally important steps in the process. To be fair, preparing for survey administration and the creation and distribution of manager reports is a huge amount of work. It's no wonder the survey team wants a break after the crush of administrative tasks required to plan the process, administer the survey, produce reports, and analyze the data.

However, organizations that elect to run a survey must commit to acting on the results. What's more, this commitment must start at the very beginning of the survey planning process—and must guide the survey strategy, the survey questions, the report design, the data analysis and interpretation training provided to HR business partners and managers, and the briefings provided to senior leaders. The expectation that the survey process will drive change needs to be communicated early and often, to all who will use the results.

When it comes right down to it, if the survey questions aren't actionable, it's very difficult to take action. If managers don't understand how to make sense of their data, create a plan, or communicate results to their employees, it's hard for them to do anything. If the data collected in the survey aren't relevant to helping managers and employees achieve success at work, how can they be expected to take action? If HR business partners don't understand their role in the process, and don't have the skills to support managers or interpret results for leaders, how can they be expected to act? And if senior leaders don't see the connection between survey results and the success of their business, if they fail to see the value of the survey in helping them achieve the organization's goals, how then can they be expected to take action?

Many senior executives and CEOs reference their company's survey program in speeches or interviews. They talk about their engagement metric, their response rate, how often they conduct the survey. They talk about how they read every comment that employees wrote, hundreds of pages. That's great; they listened. But what did they do? What was different? How did it influence their decisions, actions, and strategy? What changed as a result of the survey? Did they see the survey not just as the "right thing to do" but as a key strategic tool for leading the business?

For surveys to achieve their potential to improve organization effectiveness, organizations must:

- Have a clear strategy for the survey: Why are we doing a survey? What do we want to learn? How will we use the data? How does the survey support and inform the organization's strategy? How often should we conduct the survey and what methodologies (frequent pulses vs. annual, sample vs. census) should we use? Make sure the design and methodology of the survey matches the strategy and needs of the organization, and not what a survey consultant or supplier is peddling.
- View the survey process as an ongoing effort, not just a point-in-time event. Survey results should inform actions that are taken for many months after the survey. A

well-designed survey can provide a database that invites queries and study long after the survey has been conducted. Future surveys provide the opportunity to follow up on issues, assess change, and collect data on new topics that are important to the organization's success.

- Create clear role expectations; be clear about what is needed from senior leaders, HR professionals, managers, and employees. Make sure all parties understand what they are expected to contribute, how they are to use the results, and how they are to take action. While managers and leaders are generally thought of as the individuals tasked with planning and implementing actions, don't overlook the need to involve employees. Giving the responsibility solely to managers makes employees dependent on them for change. Give employees some skin in the game; encourage them to get involved and to own how things get done in the organization.

- Create survey content that not only reflects what is important to the organization but does so in a way that drives action. Leaders, managers, and employees reviewing survey results should recognize the issues assessed in the survey as relevant to their success, and be able to see a clear path from the results to the subsequent actions needed. As much as possible, avoid asking what's trendy and focus on what's important today to the organization.

- Listen with an open mind and accept that survey results are often negative. Not everything in the company is great. Some things need improvement. A survey that just focuses on feel-good issues doesn't do anyone any good. Good news often comes with bad news. Get ready to learn about organization strengths, and be open to negative feedback. Organizations prosper when they are willing to listen to constructive criticism and commit to continuous improvement.

- Communicate, communicate, communicate. Some companies that have made significant changes are frustrated to learn that employees feel nothing happened as a result of the survey. Actions were indeed taken based on survey findings, but nothing was communicated to employees to help them make the connection between how they responded to the survey and subsequent actions. Often the changes companies make are too subtle for employees to notice, or the actions happen many months post-survey. Employees simply don't make the connection. Employees need to be told what the changes are and, more important, why they were implemented: "We did this because of what you told us on the survey." Then tell them again. And again.

- Establish the survey as a cornerstone of a people analytics strategy. Survey data are powerful stuff, and even more so when blended with nonsurvey data. When organizations add in actual attrition, performance metrics, customer satisfaction, and sales results, they create a resource that can have an enormous influence on leaders.

The remaining chapters in this book provide greater insight and recommendations for each of these requirements. If your company has a survey program, then there is enormous potential to influence the organization in profound ways. It's not difficult. If a survey program is already in place, you are well on your way.

3

IT STARTS WITH YOUR STRATEGY

I have worked with hundreds of companies in my career, advising them on best practices for survey design, administration, analysis and action. I can honestly say that I have never done the same survey twice, and the reason is clear. No two companies are the same. Each company has its own culture and language, its own history and challenges, its own philosophy for running the business and dealing with employees. Each company has its own strategy and objectives.

Whenever I work with a new client, the first question I always ask is, "Why do you want to conduct a survey? What are you trying to accomplish?" I might also ask about what they wish to learn, what they want to know that they don't know today, or how they want to use the survey data. What I want the company to understand is the why: Why is it surveying employees?

It seems like a simple question, but you might be surprised at the number of organizations that struggle to produce an answer. Surveys have become ubiquitous in organizations, a common expectation on the part of both leaders and employees. It's easy to administer a survey, with dozens of firms happy to help any interested company by supplying their proprietary model of engagement, accompanied by predesigned sets of survey questions and stock reporting formats. Other suppliers license survey administration tools to organizations, providing a self-service survey option. Technology is easily acquired online, giving anyone the ability to construct and field a survey at any time. Given the relative ease of the process, particularly with advances in technology, the "what" or "how" of survey administration is sometimes easier to answer than the "why."

Why Conduct a Survey?

Some companies conduct an organizational survey as a check-the-box exercise. They believe it is something they need to do, because surveys have become standard in so many companies and a best practice among leading organizations. Leaders and HR staff have read enough about employee engagement to know they need to collect feedback from employees via a survey. They might make the existing survey process a predictable event in the corporate year, ingrained into their culture. But beyond this notion that a survey is something the company should do, or something the company always does, little thought is given to what leaders want to learn from the survey and how they want to use the survey data.

The "why" is critical to the success of the survey and the organization's ability to use the data in a way that enhances organization effectiveness and employee engagement. Without a clear purpose, the survey will measure topics that either are irrelevant to leaders and employees or don't lend themselves to driving action. This leads to a perception that management is out of touch with what is going on in the company, the survey is a waste of time, and that employees' feedback is not of value. Why bother conducting a survey if nothing really changes as a result?

"Evaluating employee engagement" is a good start to answering the question of why, but it isn't nearly enough. Why is engagement important to the success of the organization? That seems like an easy question to answer, right? After all, research has demonstrated that employee engagement drives all manner of business performance outcomes, from sales and revenue to customer satisfaction. So naturally every company wants high levels of employee engagement.

But beyond higher engagement, what is the company trying to achieve? Is it to be an innovator and first to market with new products? To be the low-cost provider of goods or services? To provide world-class customer service? There are, of course, many other potential objectives to which organizations can aspire. The point is that each requires different organizational operating models, different types of employees, different structures, processes, and outcomes. More important, each requires different data, insights, and guidance, much of which could be collected via an employee survey. Given all that, it is reasonable to conclude that different needs for data require different survey questions, methodologies, and analytics. The wide variety of insight needed by organizations would lead to the conclusion that there is no single approach to surveying that would be equally effective across all organizations.

Why is any of this important if the company is primarily interested in employee engagement? Isn't employee engagement relevant regardless of the organization's objective? Of course it is, but the path to engagement will vary considerably depending on the organization's industry, work processes, locations, and employees. But beyond that, the bigger issue is the role of the survey within the organization, and the strategic value that the survey may or may not have, depending on how it is positioned.

The Contribution to Organizational Success

For decades, the human resources function has aspired to be a strategic partner to the C-suite. HR has long wanted a seat at the table, and the ability to influence the direction and success of the organization via employee policies and practices. This is a worthy objective, and one that will have a positive and productive influence on an organization's success. But to be a true strategic partner, HR functions need to be able to demonstrate their value to the success of the organization by operationalizing their contribution. They must be able to show how policies and practices affect the bottom line using hard and unequivocal metrics. And that means HR needs to be able to access and use data.

Surveys can provide the data that HR functions need to become strategic partners with senior leaders. Few organizational processes can match the scope of an organization survey. Surveys can capture data from every employee in all parts of the organization, regardless of geographic location, subunit, or role. Surveys capture employee feedback on their work experience, as well as all manner of demographic data, ranging from tenure, to job title, to potential, to which internal development experiences employees have had. Surveys can provide databases that are both wide and deep and that, if well designed, can be mined over and over to respond to queries about strategic human resources issues. Surveys can cover a multitude of topics beyond employee engagement and its drivers, providing specific insights leaders need to make data-based decisions about people.

But none of this can happen without clarity on the purpose of the survey. What does the organization need to know about people to be successful?

This all requires thinking broadly and strategically about surveys in the organization, and beyond the notion that the survey is strictly about employee engagement. It involves engaging leaders in the process of creating the survey strategy, and using organization strategy and objectives as a starting point for the development of survey content and the number, type, and sequence of surveys to be administered.

Including senior leaders in the survey strategy process serves a dual purpose. First, interviews of senior leaders can yield useful insights that can be used to design the survey process, content, and analytics. Second, they provide an opportunity to expand leaders' thinking and broaden their understanding of how surveys can be used in the organization to inform decision making. These conversations can educate leaders about the value of the organization's survey beyond simply providing scorecards of engagement results, and grow their interest in the process.

Leaders involved in early stages of survey development will look forward to the survey administration and reporting process, and can more ably speak to the company's leadership and employees about the survey and the value it carries for the organization. They become true partners, invested in the process and its outcomes. Most important, they begin to see the organization's survey and the insights it produces as important tools for helping them successfully lead the organization. The resulting data and insights from the survey will enable the HR function to contribute to organization success by providing the data and insights that leaders need, and to truly have a seat at the table.

A Compelling Survey Strategy

This may all sound very complicated, but I can assure you that it isn't. In fact, creating a survey strategy can make the rest of the survey process relatively simple. The survey strategy establishes parameters for the project and streamlines decision making. The strategy defines which questions are relevant for the survey, as well as which employees should be included in the survey and how frequently they should be surveyed. The strategy will guide decisions over what management groups or levels should have access to the data and which data they should or should not receive. It guides analyses of the results and what happens post-survey.

The bottom line is that survey strategy drives the methodology of the survey; it represents the "why," which influences the "what" and the "how." Implementing a survey program in an organization without a clear understanding of the "why" will create work for many with true benefit for very few. It is the equivalent of taking an action with no clear understanding of the need for the action or the desired result. It is a wasted effort, but more significant, it is a wasted opportunity.

To develop a compelling survey strategy for the organization:

- **Brush up on the organization's business strategy and long-term plans.** What are the goals of the organization? What has been communicated to employees and investors? Does the culture of the organization need to change and adapt to achieve the strategy?

- **Understand the potential barriers to achieving the business strategy:**
  - **Marketplace challenges.** Do employees understand the needs of their customers? Do they have access to regular customer feedback? Are they aware of competitors and their products and services? How do the organization's products and services stack up to the competition?
  - **HR challenges.** There are many potential issues here, such as the organization's ability to access and retain critical talent, capabilities of managers and leaders, and development and career growth within the organization.

- ○ **Cultural challenges.** Organization culture is little more than company-wide collections of habits and behaviors. Asking the right questions about these behaviors can identify cultural barriers to change and effectiveness. Does the organization embrace risk, or is it averse to implementing new ideas and processes? How adaptable are employees and work processes? How open are employees and leaders to feedback, and is there honest communication at multiple levels of the organization? Are employees empowered to make decisions, or is there an extensive review and approval process in place?

- **Interview key organization leaders.** These interviews serve multiple purposes. The first is to collect leaders' perspectives on important strategic initiatives, what insights from employees would be most valuable, and how they would like to use survey data. The second purpose is to educate leaders on what the organization survey can do for the organization beyond measuring engagement. Interviews will provide useful insight for survey design (both the methodology and content) and will engage leaders in the process. Keep the interviews short (30 minutes works well) and relatively open ended. Plan a few questions, but let the leaders' thoughts and comments guide the discussion. Prepare some examples of the strategic use of surveys to open leaders' thinking and inspire their ideas of how they would like to use the data.

- **Outline the purpose, general content, and methodology of the survey program.** Don't move to the question-writing stage just yet. Consider what types of surveys should be used. Will a census survey provide the needed data, or is there a need for pulse surveys? What topics will be included in each? What demographic data are needed for the analysis, and what performance metrics will be needed to link survey results to business performance?

- **Develop a communications strategy for sharing this information across the HR function and with leaders.** These communications will help shape their expectations of the upcoming survey and the purpose of the survey in the organization.

A well-thought-out survey strategy can elevate an organization's survey from a routine exercise to a source of research and insight that inspires the right actions to drive organization success. The survey is no longer a project, something that is implemented and, once completed, put away for another year. A strategic survey process is the engine of an HR analytics program.

4

SURVEY STRATEGY DRIVES FREQUENCY

The administration process for organization surveys has long been influenced by the technology on hand at the time. In the early days of surveys, paper and pencil administration was the only means available, with results initially hand tabulated, and eventually scanned, into databases. Employees self-reported demographic data such as job type and tenure, and surveys used an often-complex sequence of questions to identify employees' work location and place in the organizational hierarchy. Reports were printed as well, delivered many weeks or months after the administration of the survey was completed, due to the labor-intensive process of compiling the data, analyzing them, and then printing and distributing the findings.

As technology evolved, so too did the survey administration process. Web-based tools provided the ability to collect employee responses via computers. Manager reports, though still precalculated and static, were distributed electronically. Until this point employee surveys were anonymous, meaning that the only information we had about respondents was what employees provided in their responses to demographic and organization hierarchy questions. Eventually surveys moved from anonymous to confidential, as employee data feeds from human resource information systems were uploaded and matched with employees' survey responses to provide more accurate demographic and hierarchical data.

Today, real-time reporting systems allow survey teams to track response rates and survey results as they are collected, and for manager reports to be available as soon as survey administration has ended. Technology has simplified and streamlined the survey administration process substantially, and enabled the customization of survey design, content, and reporting.

In the early days of paper and pencil administration, the prospect of conducting a single organization survey annually was daunting, and few companies considered conducting more than one survey per year, if that often. Today, technological advancements have made the survey administration process fast and efficient. These advancements in efficiency have been welcomed by those involved in the survey administration process, as it has freed more time to think strategically about the survey and provide insight and counsel to leaders. The improved accuracy of demographic data, reduced turnaround time for reporting, and greater ease of accessing and analyzing data have enhanced the understanding of critical employee and organization issues and the impact surveys can have on the organization. Streamlined processes, faster delivery of reports to leaders, and deeper analytics have enabled organizations to do more with survey data and build on the momentum created by the survey's administration. More companies are taking advantage of the increased ease of survey administration by conducting surveys more frequently, supplementing the traditional annual or biennial census survey with multiple pulse surveys.

As technology continues to evolve, the options for survey administration evolve as well, enabling virtually any type of survey with any type of design and administration frequency. More and more survey providers and researchers are touting the value of "always on" or "continuous listening" processes. These processes and tools are designed to collect data on an ongoing basis, providing a continuous stream to the organization. As it is, organizations already receive a continuous stream of data from multiple sources, whether it's customer satisfaction, sales, stock price, productivity, or hundreds of other metrics. The logic is that organizations need access to more employee data to supplement the other business metric data. Companies now seek to access and mine multiple, continuous streams of data addressing issues influencing effectiveness and success.

Continuous Listening

Like many terms in the survey world, the phrase *continuous listening* has different meanings to different professionals, but usually refers to supplementing the annual census survey with additional employee survey-based data collections. Pulse surveys, which typically feature fewer survey questions than a census survey and are administered to a subset of the organization's employees, feature strongly in continuous listening programs. In some companies, continuous listening means a daily pulse survey of employees, and in other companies, continuous listening includes conducting pulse surveys on a quarterly basis.

Continuous listening has also been used to describe employee life cycle survey programs that include a combination of census, onboarding, and exit surveys, providing insights into how employees' opinions about the organization shift from hiring to working to finally leaving the company. Regardless of how it is defined, continuous listening refers to a survey design that uses multiple surveys and designs to provide data to the organization more frequently than at a single point in a cycle, whether that cycle is biennial, annual, or shorter.

To some extent this logic makes sense; a lot can change in an organization between annual or biennial surveys, and it would be beneficial for leaders to have access to current data and analytics to help them make data-based decisions about their people. The ability to tie employee feedback to recurring metrics, whether financially or customer based, could provide valuable insights and drive performance improvements in the organization. The question, though, is what needs to be measured and how often? Just because technology can enable more surveys more frequently doesn't mean that increasing survey frequency is always a good idea.

Multiple consulting firms or survey providers have promoted the installation of a "How was your day?" button. As employees head home at the end of the day, they press either the green button ("It was a great day!") or red button ("It was a bad day!") installed by the exit. One company that used such a process determined that "Thursday was our worst day" (Celpax 2017). Other companies have instituted a "question of the day" that appears on employees' computer screens each morning; some companies require a response from employees to unlock their computers. Both tactics allow a company to collect lots of data on a frequent basis and track trends to determine how they shift over time. But do they drive insight?

Collecting data for the sake of having more data doesn't solve organizational issues, and collecting engagement data with more frequency doesn't improve employee engagement by itself. The frequency with which data are collected must be driven by need, strategy, and purpose. An organization that collects data frequently may convince itself that the act of collecting frequent data demonstrates its commitment to employees and to building organization effectiveness and employee engagement. Employees, on the other hand, care less about the frequency with which the organization collects their input, and more about how the organization acts on it. Asking employees over and over about how they feel without making any changes is like an endless, pointless loop for employees: *Why do you keep asking me if you don't do anything about it?*

One of the greatest challenges for any organization that collects employee survey data is driving action in the organization. Ask 100 companies that conduct employee surveys which step of their survey process requires the most improvement, and at least 90 would name post-survey action planning and action taking. Once survey data reports are shared in the organization, the feedback and action process becomes highly decentralized, with the next steps in the hands of hundreds, if not thousands, of managers who already have a lot on their plate. Managers may struggle to identify the issues in the survey, may feel uncomfortable sharing the survey results in a feedback session with their team, or simply may not know what actions will drive meaningful change and improvements.

So if action planning and implementation were challenges for organizations, would conducting surveys more frequently, with the subsequent ongoing stream of data, improve the situation? Likely not. In fact, more data may make organizations even less likely to act on survey data.

Say your organization collects employee survey data on a monthly or quarterly basis. While the results are always of interest to your organization's leaders, the frequency with which the data are collected and reported to them might influence their willingness and ability to act. Rather than act, they may tend to postpone decisions until more data are available. They want to see if the pattern of results held, or if the data reflected an issue that was fleeting or self-correcting. After all, if the current finding is a fluke, it may not make sense to invest time and resources into actions that may turn out to be unnecessary. At some point, the ongoing feed of survey results will evolve into solely a data analysis and tracking exercise. The notion that something needed to be done gets lost in the continuous flood of statistics. The wait-and-see approach fails to yield any more action than that from an annual census survey. Sometimes it yields no action.

This is not to suggest that frequent surveys can't be helpful to organizations; they can, assuming that the organization is conducting the right survey for the right reasons. But too many companies are being sold on a flashy new approach without fully thinking through the purpose of collecting the data. The challenge for any organization considering a continuous listening approach is to spend as much time determining why more frequent data are valuable and planning how the data will be used as it does planning the continuous administration of surveys. It is almost always a mistake to select a methodology prior to determining the data and insights needed. When methodology precedes purpose, the organization runs the risk of asking the wrong questions and collecting the wrong data, which means it will not be able to produce the insights it needs to be successful. This frustrates leaders, managers, and employees, and is a waste of resources and time. Don't choose the how before understanding the why.

So what must be considered to make a continuous listening approach a vehicle for positive change in the organization?

Purpose

Why is the organization implementing more frequent surveys? What are the milestones to which the surveys correspond? How does the frequency of survey administration fit in with organization and human resources strategies? Some areas of interest for the organization, such as reactions to rapid and ongoing organization change, or understanding the drivers of attrition, may necessitate more frequent collection of data and analysis.

Focus

What needs to be measured? What topics are of greatest value to the organization to assess frequently? Collecting employee engagement data or asking employees "How's it going?" may produce an interesting trend, but what does it really tell you? Measure the "what," whether that is employee engagement or something else, but also make sure there is a way to assess the "why." It may be interesting to know that engagement is declining, but it is insightful when the organization also has the data available to understand the reason behind the decline so that appropriate actions can be taken. Be sure to collect a balanced set of data.

Owners

Who is responsible for analyzing, understanding, and acting upon the data? Without accountability, the data will pile up, but it will not influence the organization's direction. Simply assigning owners after the data have been collected thrusts accountability onto teams and staff that didn't request the data, may not value the data they have been provided, and may not have the means to analyze the data. Identify data owners first, and involve them in the design process. How comfortable is the organization with data? Organizations with a highly analytical leader and manager population may be better owners of pulse survey data than those that are less comfortable with data analytics.

Depth

Pulse surveys tend to get lower response rates than census surveys. The difference may be due to the lower profile of pulse surveys in the organization relative to census surveys, or the fact that the pulse survey may be administered to a random sample or a subset of the employee population. Either way, the data set may not be as robust as what leaders and managers are used to in the census survey. It's natural for executives and managers to want to see results for their teams, but in many cases there may not be enough data to provide a statistically valid view of the organization, or the data cuts that provide additional insights. It is important to be realistic about the information data from a pulse survey can and cannot provide.

Impact

There can be an inverse relationship between the frequency of surveys and the employee response rate for those surveys. Employees generally are quite willing to provide their input on issues that are important to them and to the organization, particularly if they see evidence that their input drives positive change in the organization. However, organizations that survey employees repeatedly without taking action or communicating its actions effectively will see their response rates plummet. Remember, the survey process is a conversation: If only one side (employees) is participating, the conversation will shut down. Employees will choose not to participate in a process that is solely focused on collecting data with no discernable purpose.

Overall, keep in mind that it is not the frequency of surveys that is important. It is what the company does with the data, the actions and positive change that it creates based on the findings.

Census Versus Pulse Surveys

There are advantages and drawbacks for every survey design, which is why it is essential to match the right design to the right strategy or information need. I have summarized the most significant plusses and minuses in Table 4-1. Annual census surveys include feedback from employees across the organization's many subgroups and functions, yielding a database that is wide and deep and, if designed with an eye to HR and company strategy, can be queried repeatedly to understand important people and organization issues.

Table 4-1. Benefits and Pitfalls of Annual Census Versus Pulse Surveys

Daily or Frequent Pulse Surveys	Annual Census Surveys
Great for tracking a handful of data elements that can be reasonably expected to fluctuate frequently	Great for creating a wide and deep database for analytics
Can track microtrends in key metrics	Best for providing team feedback and grassroots action planning
Can be used to collect data quickly on emerging topics or follow up on census survey findings	More work for HR than a pulse survey
Less intrusive than a census survey when it comes to HR-employee involvement	Allows for tracking changes at multiple levels of the organization
Sampling doesn't allow for reporting at the manager level or of small business units	Long time gaps between data collections
Tend to get lower response rates than census surveys (20-25 percent for daily pulses)	A more visible business process

Census surveys are ideal for providing small group feedback to employees, enabling managers and their teams to connect on issues important to their success. Feedback leads to action planning and action taking, designed to address critical issues and opportunities unearthed via the survey data. This grassroots process allows employees to experience firsthand the power of their feedback and the influence they can have on the organization. When used in this manner, the census survey is a powerful tool for improving organizational effectiveness.

Census surveys are not without their disadvantages. While technology has significantly streamlined the process of census survey administration, there is a lot of work to be done to implement a census survey. Team feedback is possible only when an accurate manager reporting hierarchy has been built. Census surveys require more communication, training, and follow-up. The planning and administration process is generally longer than that for pulse surveys, because it incorporates what can sometimes be a lengthy timeline for reporting and feedback. Technology has enabled organizations to distribute data reports to managers within days of closing the survey administration, but often this process is delayed until higher levels of leaders can be briefed on the findings. Add in the need for translating survey and report content into many languages, coordinating with company IT requirements, and interacting with multiple constituent groups across the organization, and it is easy to see how managing a census survey process can be a significant undertaking.

Pulse surveys can also be valuable tools for organizations. They are a way to explore an issue uncovered in the census survey, or that is of strategic importance to the company. They can be administered to a sample of employees across the organization or to a targeted subgroup, chosen for their unique insights on key issues. Additionally, pulse surveys are usually easier and more efficient to implement given their smaller footprint, because they often don't require large communication efforts, the construction of a management hierarchy, or coordination with multiple groups across the organization. This greater ease of planning and administration can provide the opportunity to conduct pulses more frequently, either to collect more data on more topics or to provide a regular update on key metrics.

Of course, pulse surveys present drawbacks too. As mentioned, pulse surveys generally yield significantly lower response rates, because fewer employees are invited to respond and there is less communication surrounding the process. Samples and lower response rates generally mean that the data do not go as deep into the organization. Detailed data cuts by subunits or demographic groups often are not available. Administering the pulse survey to a sample of employees eliminates the opportunity to provide team-level feedback to employees, excluding them from grassroots action-planning processes. Often employees don't receive feedback on the results of pulse surveys at all, and thus cannot see the impact of their input on the organization.

None of these disadvantages, either for the census or the pulse, is fatal. Each process can be effective under the right circumstances, and they both have a place in an overall survey strategy. For instance, many companies find that a single, well-designed annual census survey is the right approach. Others link together data from multiple surveys, whether census, pulse, onboarding, or exit. And some companies have made good use of HR analytics, knitting together data from multiple surveys with employee demographics, customer satisfaction data, financial performance, attrition, and more. It all works. The challenge is to first understand the information needs of the organization. Only then can the right methodology, whether census or pulse or both, be selected. Choosing a methodology without fully considering the needs of the organization is a recipe for disaster.

Using Census and Pulse Surveys Strategically

An administration design that works for many organizations starts with an annual census survey to create a database for both manager-level feedback and action planning, as well as analytics and data-based queries about key organization issues. The census is then supplemented during the year with one or more pulse surveys that focus on a handful of critical issues identified in the census. The pulse survey may be administered to a random sample of company employees or a specific slice of the employee population, depending on the topics included in the survey. This design provides the opportunity for grassroots feedback, action planning, and deep analytics driven by the census, plus the ability to dive more deeply into specific issues and track change.

While some companies have elected to collect employee feedback data on a daily or weekly basis to maintain a continuous flow, they are few and far between. The reality is that this process is expensive to implement, and may not yield more useful information to the organization. Because only a small percentage of employees are surveyed with each administration, the data collected are not large enough to produce reports for bigger units of the organization, let alone for frontline managers. The results may suggest trends or shifts, but do not lend themselves to deep analysis to pin down where the issue exists and with which specific group of employees.

Employee surveys are valuable organization effectiveness tools. They can help organizations understand the needed pace of change. They can provide insight into employees' reactions to company events and restructurings. They can highlight support and opportunities for improvement in manager relationships, inclusion, team performance, and performance management. But for surveys to affect organization effectiveness, they need to drive actions and improvements. Employees need to understand why frequent or continuously administered pulse surveys are valuable to the organization and how their input influences the organization's decisions and actions. There needs to be more talk that centers on continuous action. It's not enough to collect the information, regardless of how well intentioned it may be. Organizations need to act on survey data to demonstrate to employees that their feedback is valuable. Not only are employees listened to; their feedback and ideas are valuable enough to influence organization policies and practices.

Use the following tips to determine how continuous listening programs, regardless of administration design, can better influence continuous acting:

- Ask insightful questions that direct action. It's not enough to just ask "How's it going?" Measure meaningful outcomes, but also collect data on factors that influence outcomes.

- Ensure that there is an owner for the data and accountability for action. Without an owner, the data cannot influence decisions, policies, or practices. Involve the owner in the design of the questions and methodology.

- Take advantage of existing company communication vehicles to update employees on the survey strategy, as well as highlights from recent pulse surveys. Describe the actions that are being taken as a result of the survey findings.

- Make it relevant. Survey data that tap into what is on the mind of senior leaders will always have more impact than data that do not have a clear use or purpose. The same goes for employees; ask them questions that reflect what is important to them.

- Does increased frequency drive insight? Will more frequent assessment of the issue add to your understanding of it? Some issues don't need to be tracked frequently to be critical focus areas for change. The best metrics to track frequently are those that are reactive, to either an event or other actions.

There is no one-size-fits-all process or methodology in the survey world. A survey strategy and administration process that is ideal in one organization could be a disaster in another. Deep analytics that excite and inspire leaders in one company could bewilder leaders at a different one. Thanks to technology, the options for employee surveys are nearly endless. The challenge for survey professionals and human resources is to determine the survey format and cadence most likely to create insight and inspire action in the organization.

5

MAKE YOUR SURVEY DYNAMIC

What do organizations as varied as chemical manufacturers, financial clearinghouses, cable and Internet providers, diamond jewelers, and airlines have in common? They all employ skilled people, they all have organization structures, they all deal with customers, and they are all in business to be successful. Each of them has an organization culture and history, and all wrestle with the issues of competition, regulation, and technology. These similarities cover only part of the things all organizations have in common.

It is what's below the surface of these organizations that makes them interesting. Yes, they all require skilled staff, but different skills, talents, and demographics. Their customer sets are vastly different, ranging from large institutions to teenagers. They exist in different marketplaces and with dramatically different levels of competition. They have their own culture and history; some have existed for only a few years, and others incorporated more than 100 years before. Even companies competing in the same market for the same customers can be enormously different from one another, like Amazon and just about any other brick-and-mortar retail organization.

If we recognize these differences and even celebrate them as differentiators for marketing or employee recruiting efforts, why would engagement survey designs, content, and processes not be as distinct from organization to organization?

Just as each organization is unique, each survey process, from the questions asked to the look and feel of the survey to the analytics to the feedback and action, should be unique as well. If we buy into the notion that the most effective employee surveys are inspired by company strategy, and if every company has a different one, then surveys need to be different across companies. If each company has a unique blend of employee skills, work processes, development cycles, and customer types and exists in a unique market, why would we ask the same questions of all of them? Why would we assume that those workplace elements important in a research lab are the same as those in a fast food restaurant? Why would we produce the same types of reports? Why would we research the same issues? Why would we think that engagement looks and feels the same?

The Downsides to a Standardized Approach

Plenty of suppliers and consulting firms seek to sell a standardized approach to survey content, comprising a set of questions to be used as-is: No changes are required, encouraged, or even allowed. These products are purported to be valid measures of employee engagement and its most common drivers. The value of these predeveloped, off-the-shelf surveys is their efficiency (no need to invest in time-consuming or costly development), their science (development is often based on engagement research conducted in academia or across hundreds, if not thousands, of companies), and their comparability (compare against benchmarks to determine percentile standard relative to other companies). These are powerful selling points.

So what are the downsides? With increased efficiency comes decreased customization. Does the language used in the survey questions make sense in the context of the organization? Are the questions appropriate given the audience? Scientific research across a variety of companies produces a broad database that will generalize the overall findings in a way that may mask patterns specific to certain industries, regions of the world, and employee types.

Similarly, benchmark data from so many types and sizes of organizations may provide a reference that represents little. Besides, the purpose of the survey is not to rank one company relative to another, but to identify strengths and opportunity areas, inform strategy, and implement targeted action.

Companies should be encouraged to take the predeveloped set of questions and tweak them, drop some, or supplement others with additional questions. While that may be frustrating to the consultant looking to provide a standardized approach, it is the right thing to do. Your company is not like any other company, so your survey should not be like that of any other company.

Remember, it's important to link survey content to organization strategy to not only engage senior leaders in the survey process but also provide organizations with data that drive change, improve organization effectiveness, and influence employee engagement. Given the variety of organization strategies, it is easy to see how standardized survey content, or even a standardized engagement metric, would not provide the data that leaders need. While standardized content may have advantages in the short term, in the long term the lack of relevant data may turn leaders off and limit their interest in the survey program.

While it may take longer to develop custom survey content—and may frustrate those in the organization who want to get data as soon as possible—the quality of data received will be well worth the investment. Besides, you don't have to start with a blank sheet of paper. Focus on the factors that are known influencers of an effective workplace and the components of engagement to provide a general framework for survey content development. What remains is interpreting those components in the current context of the organization, what the desired end state or culture is for the organization, and how to word the questions so they are understandable to those taking the survey and interpretable to those analyzing the results.

What About External Benchmarking?

All that considered, the advantage to predeveloped survey content is the availability of external benchmarks or normative data through vendor databases. The list of questions with benchmark data is generally extensive, reflecting many topics and variations of common survey questions. When a client includes one of these questions in their organization's survey, the vendor can supply the benchmark results in reports.

Benchmarks provide useful external context for interpreting survey data. They allow users of survey data to determine if their organization's scores were more favorable than, less favorable than, or about the same as the external reference point. Without such data, a determination of where there are trouble spots or strengths within the organization can be a challenge, particularly when there are no historical data for the organization to use as internal context.

However, not every question on every survey requires an external benchmark, and by no means should the interest in benchmark data dictate survey content development. In my experience, the perceived requirement for benchmarks is driven mostly by a numbers-focused survey process, meaning that leaders are too fixated on how many points separate their organization from the benchmark, rather than on what the survey has to say about how the organization functions. A small number of benchmark questions covering some of the questions in major survey categories will give a sense of whether the organization is leading or lagging. Ultimately, the organization's own history, improvements, and declines in survey scores will provide the most valuable source of context for identifying where action has reaped benefits and where additional effort is required.

Each organization requires a unique perspective on the issues that are most important to its success. It would seem obvious that many necessary survey topics and questions have not been included on other surveys and therefore have no external benchmark comparisons. Every survey requires some custom development of content, and will benefit from some degree of tailoring to capture the data that reflect what is most important to the organization.

Although benchmarks can be helpful interpretation tools, their use requires a tradeoff between the benefits of having external context data on a generic question versus the insight gained from a question designed to reflect the organization's unique issues. You can make a case for both approaches, and including a mix of standard and custom questions in a survey is truly the best of both worlds.

Tracking Trends Versus Customizing Content

One of the great values of surveys is the ability to assess employee and organization trends quantitatively and objectively. The same survey questions asked repeatedly over time provide the opportunity to evaluate trends in the data, which in turn provide insights into whether survey actions have had the desired impact.

Does that mean that survey content, once established, can't be changed? The notion of maintaining survey content to track change over time and the desire to evolve survey content from survey to survey may seem at odds with each other. Once an organization completes the customized development of its survey content, it is natural to want to readminister that content year after year, or survey after survey. The logic behind this is sound, particularly if the survey content reflects core values and critical topics that influence organization effectiveness. Why would a company choose to change the categories and questions in its survey?

But as economies, markets, technology, customer needs, and regulations change, so must organizations. These shifts are not just external to the organization; an organization's structure, leadership, culture, values, and administration change as well. Organizations that fail to adapt to their environment are destined to become obsolete.

The same can be said of survey content. As the organization changes, some once-important issues may fade away and new issues emerge in their place. You and the survey project team must be willing to let go of previous survey content and trend data to help the organization improve. Survey questions and topics that fail to evolve with the organization will result in the survey process and its results becoming outdated. Organization changes yield new information needs, which can only be met with new survey content and analytics.

The challenge for most organizations is not so much understanding the need for new content as the need to let go of old content. There is typically great interest in developing new questions to assess new issues, because it is seen as strategically scratching the organization's itch for fresh insights. What is more difficult is convincing some leaders and staff groups to give up questions that may no longer be relevant to the organization.

But beyond potentially rendering the survey obsolete, an additional problem arises when you hold on to certain survey questions and historic data trends: the validity of historical data in the context of an evolving organization. Organization changes that involve restructuring, mergers, acquisitions, divestitures, significant hiring of new staff, or shedding of current staff via layoffs can result in an organization that looks very different from its previous incarnation. Given shifts in the size or makeup of the employee population, new structures, and new lines of business, is the present even comparable to the past? Is it the same company, and if not, is the historical trend valid?

Many companies, when faced with this situation, choose to forgo historical comparisons. This is a realistic choice; any attempts to draw conclusions based on comparisons would be seen as meaningless or misleading. When the organization has been through a significant transformation, it is generally best to start fresh with data collection, and put aside any previous trends in the data.

But acknowledging that shifts in the organization's structure and employee population might render trends obsolete does not necessarily mean that there is a similar break with the list of questions used in the survey content. After all, just because the data for the current organization cannot be compared with the previous organization structure, it does not mean that the questions need to change. Why is it necessary to let go of questions that have been useful in the past?

Certain survey questions can be seen as unchangeable for several reasons. First of all, some questions measure fundamental constructs that remain relevant despite significant changes in the organization. These topics are still central to the goals of the organization, so it makes sense to continue their use in future surveys. When considering what to keep, delete, or edit from previous survey's content, it is generally best to keep the questions measuring constructs that reflect ongoing and fundamental issues, such as employee engagement, company values (assuming they have remained the same amid structural changes), and confidence in the future of the organization. It may also be argued that topics such as the job, teamwork, and managers remain relatively the same despite organizational changes.

Some survey questions or indexes become quite beloved, either by a staff group or senior leaders. For example, the diversity and inclusion staff may consider questions that comprise an inclusion index to be unchangeable because there is a long-term goal to enhance diversity and inclusion in the organization. Certain questions about managers may be used in a business unit to evaluate talent, and given the importance of the data to this initiative, the business may insist that these questions continue to be included in future surveys. The head of the staff responsible for ethics and compliance may wish to retain a specific set of questions on the survey to provide data on inclusion to the board of directors or an external watchdog group. Some leaders simply like the way a question is worded and believe it provides a valuable piece of information that should not be lost.

When You Don't Need Trend Data

So if some survey questions must continue because they measure fundamental issues, and leaders or staff groups in the organization have staked their claim to other questions as unchangeable, how can the survey keep pace with the changes to the organization? Ultimately this is a choice between trends and relevance. Trend data are indeed valuable, but if retaining the trend means that the organization has to settle for data that are less relevant, it is a poor tradeoff indeed.

Just as not every question included in a survey needs an external benchmark comparison, not every survey question needs historical data to provide valuable insight. It is often necessary to argue that a particular topic or issue has been included in the survey through enough iterations to provide insight and trends, and the organization needs to let go of the topic for the time being. A single set of data for an issue can provide enough insight to drive meaningful actions, and the success of actions is often better assessed through evaluations other than survey results.

The purpose of survey action planning and implementation is not to get a better score on the next survey. In fact, in many cases there are arguably more relevant and valid metrics of effective change than whether the score on a survey question has changed over time.

For example, consider the topic of ethical compliance and willingness to report violations of ethical conduct. Many companies choose to include questions on this topic in their survey and track the trends. Instead of using survey responses to evaluate whether actions to inform employees about ethical guidelines are effective, why not track the percentage of employees who have participated in ethical training, or the shift in the number of ethical violations reports?

Or, consider diversity and inclusion topics. In lieu of asking employees year over year whether they believe their company supports a diverse workplace, track diversity hiring and the upward movement of diverse candidates in the organization, or even the external programs that the organization sponsors to create interest in the company or its field among diverse populations.

In many instances, opinion data from employees may not be the best indicator of meaningful change. Actions are undertaken to change the work environment, alter the way work gets done, or drive organization outcomes, not just to change employees' opinions. Objective criteria—what's different in the organization as a result of actions—is generally the better metric. Employee opinions do still matter; organizations want to understand if employees see changes and appreciate the effort they've made to change. However, opinions should not be the sole metric of success, because employee opinions often lag behind changes in the organization.

What Message Does Your Survey Content Send?

There is a bigger issue with survey content than just the ability to trend results or benchmark externally, and that revolves around the message that survey content sends to employees and managers.

Organization surveys are a primary tool for employees to communicate with leaders, with the organization asking questions, employees responding, and leaders listening and (hopefully) acting. But the survey process itself—the questions asked, the look and feel of the questionnaire and manager reports, the way the data are used—communicates a great deal to your employees about what leaders think is important. Survey content that is viewed as not reflective of current issues in the organization, or never changes survey after survey, may lead employees to think that leaders are out of touch with the reality in the trenches. An organization that is in the midst of difficult change, yet asks the same questions that were asked in better, more stable days, may be viewed by employees as unfeeling, unaware, and tone-deaf to their challenges. Altering survey content to reflect and support organization changes and topical issues can reinforce changes the organization is trying to make.

A recent client of mine was in the middle of a significant transformation of its business and culture. Like many other companies, this organization was shedding its more traditional business units and attempting to enter new markets that were more technologically focused. It recognized that these strategic changes required supporting cultural changes, and therefore implemented a number of initiatives to change the way employees approached their tasks and made decisions. It promoted working in fluid teams that spanned organization functions. Requirements for multiple levels of reviews and approvals before a decision could be made were greatly relaxed. It completely revised its performance management and pay and recognition systems to encourage and reward the new ways of working.

This company wisely recognized that to truly change the culture of the organization, it needed to change long-held work habits. And one of its longest-held habits was the company-wide employee survey. The survey had been an annual event in the organization for nearly 20 years, and had been a significant source of data and insight for leaders. The content of the survey had evolved over the years to reflect ongoing organization changes, but the way the results were analyzed and used had become ingrained. HR business partners and local HR teams were the primary drivers of the analysis, consulting with the leaders they supported to parse the data, communicate the findings, and plan and implement actions. These actions were implemented from relatively high levels in the organization.

These practices—habits, really—seemed out of touch with the new direction of the organization. Employees were expected to be the drivers of change in the new culture, not senior leaders. Given the dramatic shift in what the company was all about, the topics included in previous surveys and the follow-up processes used represented old habits, and not the new behaviors that the organization was attempting to drive. The survey became a symbol of what the organization used to be, not what it aspired to be.

As a result, the organization completely redesigned every aspect of the survey process to be consistent with its new strategy and direction, and to signal the new direction of the organization to employees. The list of survey questions was slimmed down from more than 45 to 12, all of which focused on team and employee behavior. Gone were questions that asked about pay, benefits, managers, training, ethics, inclusion, and other topics. The new set of questions was driven by what was most important to the organization in that moment: Are we adopting the new work behaviors that will help us succeed? The survey process was dramatically streamlined to move very quickly, another cultural tenet and behavior that the company was trying to instill. The survey was open for administration for just one week, and reports were available within 72 hours of the survey's closing. Rather than send data reports to managers, who were to share the results with employees and then plan and implement actions, data reports were sent directly to all employees, regardless of whether they completed the survey. The message was clear: It was no longer the manager's job to interpret the issues raised in the survey and take action. Employees were expected to drive change in the organization, and were being given the tools to do so. In addition to the data report, employees received a short guide that helped them interpret the report and provided suggestions on how to work within their team to enhance their performance.

HR business partners were no longer responsible for interpreting survey results to business leaders, as the reports were quite simple and straightforward. Leaders were no longer responsible for fixing problems, but were instead tasked with determining what they might be doing that stood in the way of employee and team performance. After all, they needed to adopt new behaviors as well.

The redesigned survey process successfully encouraged new thinking and changed behaviors in a way that was consistent with the new strategy and direction of the organization. Retaining the legacy survey content and process in the context of the new strategy would have sent a confusing message to leaders and employees and could have hampered the cultural changes the organization was seeking.

This example reflects an extreme change in survey design, and not all companies are prepared to imitate it. However, it demonstrates that when an organization is undergoing a shift in its culture, it often requires a shift in many ongoing processes, including the survey. Retaining survey content from administration to administration does indeed provide some value to organizations, but it is essential for the organization to consider the implications of continuing to use the same survey content year over year.

How to Create Custom Survey Content

The thought of writing survey questions and determining reporting content may feel daunting. What to ask? How to ask it? What makes for a good survey question? But it is not as difficult as it may seem.

Use senior leader interviews to collect insight into the most critical topics for the organization. What specifically do leaders need to know about the organization and employees? These findings will help shape the direction and focus of the survey design. It will be necessary to go deeper than topic headings, such as efficiency, to create meaningful content. Focus on the behavioral elements of the topic to write the best questions.

Review past survey results to understand strengths and opportunities for the organization. Where would additional and more specific data further clarify an issue? When reviewing survey data, pay close attention to questions with large neutral scores, such as those in the middle of the scale. Large neutral scores often indicate that a question is not clearly written or well understood. If you have included a "Not Applicable" response option in the response scale, pay close attention to those questions with the highest percentage of employees who chose that option; the question may reflect a topic that is irrelevant to employees.

Consider where benchmark data would and would not be useful. Benchmark data are useful for global organizations, as survey results are significantly affected by country culture. The ability to compare results for your employees in Japan with an external benchmark for Japan will prevent a common data misinterpretation. On the other hand, if an issue is very specific to your organization, the ability to compare with an average may not be meaningful or even possible. Some companies I have worked with have adopted a viewpoint that they are the benchmark for other companies, and focus only on whether survey results meet internal expectations.

Keep language very simple; a good rule of thumb is to write to an eighth-grade reading level, although this can be adjusted to reflect company employees. Avoid cultural idioms and jargon that are not widely understood. Simply worded questions will translate more accurately into other languages. Focus each question on a single thought and avoid double-barreled questions. It may seem efficient to ask, "I understand and live by the company's values," but the results will be difficult to interpret. Do they understand more, less, or the same as they live by the values? The answer cannot be determined by this question. Use simple, declarative statements. Negatively worded questions ("I never think about leaving the company") are difficult to interpret and will confuse managers and leaders.

Use a five-point response scale with a neutral midpoint. A lot has been written over the years about the merits of different point scales over the years. The five-point scale is the most universally used and understood. It provides enough data points to facilitate research and analytics and gives people the opportunity to respond that they are neither favorable nor unfavorable, which is a legitimate opinion that needs to be captured in the data and respected by the organization.

Send different report designs to different data users. Develop categories of users, whether those are first-line managers, leaders of leaders, HR business partners, headquarters staff, or senior executives of a large business unit or region. What information does each need or, perhaps more important, not need? In general, it is helpful to provide just enough data, as opposed to providing lots of data without a clear strategy for how they will be used or what insights they provide. Giving a lot of data to users simply because they are available does not provide greater benefits or insights. Create multiple report templates that provide the right amount of data to the right user.

Your objective needs to be developing a survey program that has lasting value to the organization. Lasting value is a product of strategically relevant survey content that provides unique insights and drives meaningful change that enhances organization effectiveness. The best way to achieve this objective is to develop customized survey content and reporting that reflects the uniqueness of the organization and its information needs. Every component of the survey process—from the topics addressed to the technology used to the results reported—sends a message to the organization. Custom development of critical survey-process components ensures that the message truly reflects the organization and is not generic.

Where to Begin?

It isn't necessary to start with a blank sheet of paper when designing survey content for each survey administration, but there are some good practices to follow:

- Good survey design includes a core set of questions that reflect the topics that are fundamental to organization success, such as employee engagement and organizational values. This core set of questions bears repeating survey after survey to monitor the fundamentals.
- Surround the core questions with additional questions on topics that are of current relevance to the organization and successful implementation of strategic initiatives. These topics may be continued over several administrations and then retired to make way for new topics.
- Survey content should be cohesive and tell a coherent story through the combination of topics and questions.

Surveys that are an amalgamation of legacy questions and pet topics of staff groups and senior leaders can take on a "kitchen sink" quality, collecting loads of data but not communicating an overall message.

- Consider survey content from the perspective of multiple constituent groups. What message does the collection of survey questions and topics send to employees and managers? Does it accurately reflect the issues they are currently dealing with, or does the survey continue to comprise questions that feel out of touch with reality?

- Evaluate the tradeoff between continuing to collect trend data on legacy questions and collecting data on new topics of interest to the organization. Does continuing the trend add additional value and insight to leaders? Is it a nice to have, rather than a need to have?

An organization's survey is a unique opportunity to collect valuable data that can supply grassroots feedback and fuel an analytics strategy that helps leaders make data-based decisions about people in the organization. Organizations change, as do their needs for insight and information. The survey needs to change as well to keep pace and remain a valuable tool for leaders.

6

GETTING TO THE "WHY" OF ORGANIZATION EFFECTIVENESS

The construct of employee engagement has become ubiquitous in surveys, and for many organizations it is the primary focus of the survey. Engagement is typically measured via a defined set of survey questions, and engagement scores can be calculated for any subunit, team, or demographic group defined in the organization's hierarchy. Engagement scores can provide a helpful metric for the organization. The scores can be tracked over time to determine change, and can be compared with external benchmarks to determine if the organization's scores are within an expected range or significantly ahead of or behind the pack.

The ability to deliver a standard metric across so many components of the organization naturally invites comparisons. Organizations use these scores to compare business units, leaders, and managers, and some organizations include engagement metrics in manager performance goals. Engagement scores have been shared with teams in feedback sessions, posted on bulletin boards in break rooms, and presented to boards of directors. The "what" of engagement, meaning the number used to describe the current state, receives a tremendous amount of attention.

Employee engagement is an outcome measure, meaning that engagement is a product of many potential influences, such as the work itself, company culture, confidence in the organization's future, opportunities for growth and development, and employees' relationships with their managers. If the organization's objective is to increase employees' level of engagement, it is necessary to understand which factors have the greatest influence on levels of engagement—or thought of another way, which factors are barriers to high engagement and success.

It is difficult to determine which action will be most effective if you don't know what is influencing the problem. You need to understand more than just the "what" of employee engagement—you need to understand the "why" as well to design and implement meaningful and effective actions.

Without understanding the "why" of engagement, organizations run the risk of making significant investments in actions that while well intended, do little or nothing to affect employee engagement. Worse, some organizations may simply focus on the engagement metric, racking and stacking managers without giving a lot of thought as to what elements of the workplace are engaging or disengaging.

Holding leaders and managers accountable for engagement without providing the insights necessary to improve engagement seems futile and unfair.

To understand the why of engagement, some organizations focus actions on topics that received the lowest scores in the survey. While this approach seems perfectly logical, it can be flawed. Some survey categories and questions typically receive low scores, regardless of engagement levels in the organization.

One common example is compensation and benefits. Low scores in this category are the norm, even in organizations with high levels of engagement. Competitive pay and benefits are necessary in organizations, but research indicates that they are not meaningful influences on engagement. The Corporate Leadership Council's 2004 research into the drivers of engagement found that compensation wasn't even among the top 50 drivers of engagement. Further, research by Josh Bersin and Deloitte (2015) found that compensation is a "hygiene" factor, meaning that employees may leave a company if compensation is too low, but it doesn't directly drive engagement. Investing time and effort on this topic may provide a temporary boost to employee engagement, but it won't last. It simply isn't a meaningful barrier to success for the company or the individual. Other companies have implemented actions that strive to make the workplace fun, providing seemingly endless supplies of coffee, pizza, doughnuts, and even alcohol. Still others distribute a barrage of certificates of appreciation. And yet engagement remains unchanged.

A company I once worked with invested heavily in improving flexible work arrangements, the lowest-rated question in its survey. After investing resources to design, implement, and communicate new programs for employees, subsequent surveys showed that engagement was unchanged. This was extremely disappointing to leaders, because they thought they were doing the right thing.

This all leads to a simple conclusion: They are trying to fix the wrong problem. Without understanding the factors that influence engagement, action plans become a shot in the dark, a presumption of what might improve engagement, but with no proof or support that the approach will have any positive impact. These failed attempts at implementing actions to improve engagement may discourage leaders from taking further actions or, even worse, lead them to decide that the survey is a waste of time. Some leaders profess that engagement is a personality trait, meaning that employees are naturally engaged or disengaged. Consequently, leaders are helpless to do anything to improve engagement levels in the company. Because organizations don't have endless budgets for implementing actions, they need to understand the why of engagement to implement actions that address the issues that truly influence engagement.

Driver Analysis

There are many approaches to identifying workplace factors that influence employee engagement scores, a process commonly known as driver analysis. A driver analysis is simply a statistical method for identifying which survey results have the strongest relationship with the engagement measures used in the survey. It allows organizations to rank survey measures (categories, questions, or both) from those with the greatest influence on engagement to those with the least. Action planning can then focus on engagement levers, or those issues with the strongest relationship to engagement. Driving improvements on the issues will in turn have the greatest influence on engagement scores. This approach is not only logical, but supported by data.

Often the biggest influences on engagement are not the lowest scores on the survey. Very rarely does compensation emerge as a top driver of engagement, as I mentioned previously. Sometimes favorably rated questions are top drivers of engagement, suggesting that improving engagement requires further enhancement of issues measured in these questions, or at the very least maintaining the current focus on the issue. In this respect, a driver analysis can serve as a myth buster for leaders and others in the organization. Statistical analysis of the engagement drivers provides the facts and data needed to shape understanding of what is most important to employees. Identifying the best actions to improve organization effectiveness and employee engagement becomes a logical, data-based exercise, rather than one based on beliefs, assumptions, and gut feelings.

But how do you conduct driver analyses? What approaches and processes work best? Some approaches, such as correlation coefficients, are relatively simple, while others are more statistically sophisticated, like structural equation modeling. Each approach offers a unique perspective on the relationship between survey scores and employee engagement, and each has benefits and pitfalls. The choice of one or the other depends on how the data are going to be used and by whom (simplicity), how much time is available to do the analysis (speed), and whether the analysis can be efficiently conducted for multiple groups throughout the management hierarchy (scalability).

Here is a brief rundown on the most common methods of driver analysis.

Correlation Coefficients

Correlation coefficients describe how two metrics move in relation to each other. Does one increase as the other increases? Do they decrease together? Does one improve as the other declines, or is there no discernible relationship between the two? Correlation coefficients describe whether the metrics move in the same or different directions, and how closely the movements in the two metrics mirror each other. Correlation coefficients are relatively common statistics; one of the benefits of using them is that leaders and managers generally understand them. They are scalable, meaning they are easy to produce not only for the total company but also for multiple subgroups such as business units, regions, and lower levels of management. There are many software programs that can calculate correlation coefficients, and in general the analysis can be completed quickly.

But correlation coefficients have a significant disadvantage: They describe the relationship, but they do not confirm causality, meaning we cannot assume that one metric causes or influences the other. For example, a correlation coefficient may show that as scores for a survey question on flexible work arrangements improve, so do scores for the employee engagement questions. That doesn't necessarily mean that flexible work arrangements have an influence on engagement. It's even possible that engagement is affecting employees' views of flexible work arrangements. Correlation coefficients describe relationships, but not in a definitive, causal way.

Relative Weights Analysis

Relative weights analysis is a form of regression analysis that is uniquely suited to work with organization survey data. One of the unique challenges of survey data is that, statistically speaking, everything is related to everything else: How we feel about our manager is related to how we feel about recognition is related to how we feel about development opportunities is related to how engaged we are. Every element of the work environment has some influence on employee engagement, but what we want to understand is which element has the greatest influence. Relative weights analysis controls for these interrelationships, and provides as its output a ranking of engagement drivers from the greatest impact to the least. Additionally, results of a relative weights analysis assess the strength of each survey element as a driver of engagement, relative to the others. This relative ranking provides insight into whether the ranked drivers are closely packed, meaning they differ from one another only slightly in their impact on engagement, or dispersed, meaning that one or two drivers have a great deal of impact and the others have very little.

On the plus side, relative weights analysis moves us closer to understanding causality, meaning the direction of the relationship between survey measures and engagement. However, there are some significant pitfalls to consider. The analysis itself is complicated, taking additional time to complete, and it can be difficult to explain to managers. Relative weights analysis also requires a large data set to produce valid results, meaning that insights will only be available to large subunits of the organization, and not at lower levels of management. Because of this group size requirement, smaller subunits will need to share the set of drivers identified at a much higher level of the organization, which may raise questions of whether results are truly generalizable across different work environments.

Structural Equation Modeling

Structural equation modeling is the most complicated and least used of the approaches to driver analysis. It brings us even closer to understanding causality, but comes with significant pitfalls. It is a time-consuming analysis to conduct, requiring an experienced user to work through multiple iterations of a model of interrelationships. Even then, results and solutions can be difficult to interpret. It is a sophisticated statistical analysis with a unique software package, and it is very difficult to explain to managers. It isn't a scalable approach, because it needs a large data set to produce valid results. Generally, structural equation modeling is used only at the total company level, for large business units (think several thousand employees), or for research purposes. Because of the many iterations required for the analysis, the turnaround time for results can be lengthy.

Positive Divergence Analysis

Positive divergence analysis divides an employee population by how individuals responded to a defined set of survey questions. In the case of an engagement index, the population is divided into two groups: those who responded favorably to all engagement index questions (the highly engaged group) and those who didn't (the less engaged group). Once the population has been divided, it is possible to see what proportion of the population is engaged; obviously, large proportions are better than small ones. We can also determine what workplace experiences differentiate the two groups the most. In other words, what are the elements of the work environment that engaged employees are experiencing, but other employees are not? This is accomplished by calculating scores on all other survey questions for each group, comparing the scores, and ranking the score differences from the largest to the smallest. This ranking provides insight into the differences between the work experiences of the highly engaged and not engaged groups, and what experiences differentiate the groups the most. The questions with the largest differences between the two groups are the primary drivers of engagement. This methodology is logical and easy to explain to managers (it is a form of best practice research) and can be run on even small groups of 25 employees, making it highly scalable. Positive divergence analysis can be programmed into survey reporting tools, making the turnaround time for the analysis very quick.

A summary of these methodologies is presented in Table 6-1. Each can have value, but it is important to consider simplicity, scalability, and speed when determining which methodology to use.

Table 6-1. Comparison of Driver Analysis Methodologies

Method	Speed Will it slow down reporting time?	Intuitive Appeal Does this make sense to users?	Scalability How many managers will receive unique results?
Correlation Coefficients	Fast	Moderate	High
Relative Weights Analysis	Slower	Lower	Moderate
Structural Equation Modeling	Slow	Low	Low
Positive Divergence Analysis	Fast	High	High

Can You Drive Engagement?

The interest in employee engagement in organizations has narrowed people's perspective on what surveys are all about and what they can accomplish in the organization. So much emphasis has been placed on achieving high engagement scores that surveys have evolved into an effort not to drive needed improvements, but to make employees feel differently about their organizations. Focusing so much on driving engagement scores pushes aside other, potentially more useful purposes of the survey. It also suggests that engagement is something that companies need to manage and control, rather than a natural reaction to the current state of the organization.

For years now, managers and leaders have talked about and thought about engagement (as it relates to employees) as a noun, a thing to be measured, tracked, and driven. The phrase *employee engagement* is a noun, to be sure, but do organizations derive the greatest insight and opportunity for improvements by thinking about engagement as a thing? Focusing on the noun drives many organizations to limit their thinking about engagement to the number, the score on their engagement index. The attention to the score often leads to setting numerically based goals for improving it, which leads to rankings of managers and leaders based on the score for their segment of the organization. None of this, in my experience, leads to any meaningful change or improvements to the organizations.

Organizations are far better off when they stop focusing on engagement as a noun, and focus their attention on *engage,* the verb. Leaders are far better served by thinking about how to engage employees rather than how to fix employee engagement. By thinking differently about the subject, HR professionals, leaders, and managers can focus on the elements of the work environment that engage employees. What experiences, cultural factors, communications, or strategies engage their hearts and minds? Which elements of the work environment engage, and which disengage? What barriers prevent employees from fully engaging with their work, their customers, and their organization? How can changes in the work experience enable them to anticipate their success in the organization?

Is this simply a semantic difference? I don't think so. Reframing "driving engagement" to "creating a work environment that engages employees" changes the way leaders think about potential actions. Rather than planning and implementing actions that are focused on making employees feel differently, actions can focus on what elements of the work environment block both the organization's success and the employees'. Leaders will think about how work, processes, policies, and relationships should be tweaked, implemented, redesigned, or eliminated to benefit both parties. It is no longer about scores and driving those scores higher on subsequent surveys. It is about getting the feedback needed to continuously improve the work environment and the way work gets done in the company. This new focus has intuitive appeal to leaders; they know how to think about work, processes, and factors that influence success. Leaders will begin to think about employees as one of the key elements to success in the business. Ensuring the success of employees drives the success of the business overall.

Employee engagement is a product of the many elements of the work environment, from employees' degree of involvement in decisions to having access to the right tools and resources to relationships with co-workers. These elements influence engagement—and organization effectiveness and productivity. The objective with surveys ought to be diagnosing the issues that stand in the way of success and implementing actions that create a more effective organization. Organizations are effective because they are engaging. Employees buy into its strategy and mission, and they relish the opportunity to be part of something that is bigger than themselves, that equips them to contribute and succeed. They can work with talented colleagues and be inspired by great leaders. Employees have the ability to grow their capabilities and their careers. They are valued by their peers and the organization, and recognized for their contributions.

Like I said in chapter 3, every organization aspires to be successful, and every organization has its own definition of success. But regardless of the definition, success is a product of performance. Different strategies require different organizational behaviors and tactics. Organizational culture and work processes are very different in a low-cost provider than in a company that provides a unique and specialized product or customer experience.

Surveys, when well designed to suit the organization's strategy, can provide valuable insights that will enhance performance, which will then drive success. A work environment that engages employees also drives organization performance.

Dozens of research studies have demonstrated that engaged employees have a strong influence on organization performance. Employees in engaging work environments are more productive, more motivated to work hard and contribute new ideas, and more likely to stay with the organization, allowing the organization to hold on to experienced talent.

So, while working for a successful and effective organization is engaging, working for a dysfunctional organization is not. Trying to "drive" engagement in a struggling and ineffective organization can be a losing proposition if you do not expand the scope of the survey beyond measuring engagement to understanding the barriers to engagement and performance in the organization.

The goal of any organization survey is to assess the specific elements of performance required to achieve success as defined by the company, and provide insights into which elements are most in need of attention. One component of that is identifying the barriers to creating an engaging work environment. What is preventing employees from fully contributing to the organization, doing their best work, and feeling as though their contributions and participation make a difference in the organization? What are the elements of the workplace that attract and retain the right talent? Survey content and analytics must uncover not only what will drive organization performance, but also the barriers to employees' success in the organization. Employees will engage with the organization to the extent that they can anticipate and achieve their desired degree of success in the organization.

What influences employee success in an organization? Their ability to advance their careers, learn and grow, do interesting and important work, contribute to the organization, feel as though they are part of something important, be recognized for her accomplishments. But these influences vary from organization to organization, and between employee groups.

For example, what influences production workers to anticipate their desired level of success can be quite different from executives' anticipation of their success. Thus, the survey needs to tease out these different influences. Because, in the end, helping employees become successful also helps the organization become successful. Engagement will come along for the ride.

Placing a greater focus on success—the organization's and employees'—and reframing the discussion from measuring employee engagement to creating a work environment that engages employees will not only yield better insights from the survey data, but encourage a more fruitful conversation with senior leaders. Most leaders understand enough about employee engagement to recognize its value to the organization, but many still struggle to see the value of the survey and survey data beyond measuring engagement and identifying drivers. If you change the survey conversation to focus more on organization success and the success of employees, the survey emerges as a source of valuable insights for improving business performance. Leaders and managers can be inspired to plan actions and implement changes when they see the connection to business success—when the survey is no longer seen as a scorecard but a strategic tool, not as an HR initiative but a resource for them to lead the organization and achieve its goals and objectives. That can make all the difference in the interest and attention paid to the process, in turn casting the survey team as a critical business resource.

To stop driving employee engagement and begin creating a workplace that engages employees to improve organization success:

- Remind managers and leaders that employee engagement scores are a means to an end, and not the end itself. The engagement score describes the extent to which the current work environment engages employees. High engagement scores mean that the company is on the right track but needs to continue to deliver on important workplace components. Low scores indicate that changes to the work environment are in order. The objective of the survey process is not to get a higher score on the next, but rather to identify where improvements are necessary and to take action.

- Recast the survey's purpose to focus on organization strategy and success. Emphasize the link between survey questions and the strategy, and present survey results to leaders in a format that reflects critical organization goals and objectives.

- Demonstrate the link between changes in the work environment and employee engagement, for better or for worse. Explain the shifts in employee engagement within the context of organization events and changes, educating leaders on how events and changes influence both engagement and organization success.

Why the "Why" Matters

Survey data can feel overwhelming to many managers. When presented with results for many survey questions and categories, not to mention engagement, managers may struggle with how to sift through the data and determine what needs action. Without guidance, they may focus their attention on low-rated questions and issues that could be out of their control, such as compensation. They may work hard to implement actions that have no impact on employee engagement. They may believe that they cannot do anything to change employee engagement levels.

You want managers to be successful when working with survey data, so it is important to provide them with insights that go beyond the "what" and explain the "why." Understanding the why leads them to practical and meaningful action plans that will make a difference to their employees and to the organization as a whole. Driver analysis provides valuable insight that managers need to move confidently to the action planning and implementation stage of the process.

Understanding the "why" behind survey results drives meaningful change in an organization and makes the survey process a catalyst for improving effectiveness. To understand the "why":

- Conduct surveys that measure more than just employee engagement. Tracking a single metric over time, regardless of how important that metric is, provides minimal information and little insight for change.
- Create survey content that reflects the common influences on employee engagement, in addition to the workplace elements and issues that are critical to the success of the organization's strategy.
- Select a driver analysis methodology that suits the organization's requirements and leaders' capabilities. Consider the need for speed in completing the analysis, and the scalability necessary to provide customized results for different parts of the organization. Which approach is simplest to explain to managers and the most credible?
- Provide driver results to managers in a format that is easy to consume, and guides them toward taking action.

Data can paint a picture of an organization at a given point in time. Responses to the questions in the survey, when compiled, describe the current state, both the positives and the negatives. While understanding the current state is essential, it is more important to understand how things got to this point: What are the elements of the work environment that have led the organization to its current level of engagement (or disengagement) and success (or lack thereof), and what can be done to improve? That is the end game for any engagement survey, and the data can show us the way forward.

7

SURVEYS FEED
PEOPLE ANALYTICS

Many factors contribute to the success of an organization's survey program. Relevance of the survey content to the organization's strategy, a survey design best suited to the purpose of the survey, and high-quality survey administration and data reporting are all necessary for maximum impact. Reviews of survey results often raise as many questions as the survey itself. What is driving this result? Are we seeing this pattern across multiple locations or divisions, or is it limited to a segment of the company? What is going on with at-risk employee groups? What does the survey tell us about our progress in cultural transformation? Or, simply, what does it all mean?

Results from well-designed and timely surveys almost always create a "light bulb" moment, when a leader or manager gains a new insight or perspective they did not have before the survey. These moments are a product of good data analysis. Well-chosen analytics drill into the body of data to combine responses to survey questions with demographics, trends, and context in a way that goes beyond presenting a simple summary of results. They provide true insight, which opens minds, changes perspectives, and busts common myths about employees that may have been long held in the organization. Data-driven insight, when delivered on a regular basis, makes the HR organization a true strategic partner to executive leadership in the organization.

It is hard to read an HR journal, attend a conference on talent management, or scan a website for any professional HR organization without seeing references to the importance of people analytics. Organizations have always collected vast amounts of data about employees, customers, business outcomes, employee and organization performance, and much more. Technological advances have made it easier to stitch different databases together so they may be analyzed to uncover patterns and relationships. Many organizations have made large investments in technology and staffing to create analytics departments tasked with corralling big data and searching for hidden patterns and connections that inform leaders' decisions. Employees are typically an organization's largest expense and their most significant influence on success. Measuring, recording, and analyzing as much data about employees as the organization can lay its hands on simply makes sense. Analysis can drive decisions based on facts and data that are most likely to pay off for the organization.

Go Beyond Your Gut

Without data, decisions are based on hunches, trends, or what the leading companies are doing. While there is some value to these as influencers of decisions, without facts and data they can be high-risk propositions. What works in some companies, leading or not, may not transfer well across other organizations and cultures. Trends are often exaggerated by media outlets or firms that stand to profit from those trends. Most gut decisions are biased by personal beliefs and assumptions. And what worked in the past may not work now, given changes in the organization or the marketplace. Providing guidance to senior leaders that is based on anything other than facts and data is risky; it's a guess about what might work or what could happen. It certainly does not portray the HR function as pragmatic and driven by business results.

Human resources functions are eager to join the data analytics movement. Corporate executives speak the language of data and analytics, so coming to the table armed with just that goes a long way in making HR a strategic partner to the business. However, many HR functions find the transformation to data-based decision making challenging. HR often does not have the analysis tools, data science or statistical talent, or database access necessary for an ongoing, high-quality analytics program. And the perceived cost of entry and time required to ramp up an analytics program seem very steep.

Fortunately, an organization's survey program provides an important entry point to a people analytics strategy. A census survey includes all employees in all units and regions of the company. It collects data for every subgroup of worker, from senior leaders to hourly employees, and from recent hires to people with 20 or more years of service. Survey results are typically linked with demographic data from the company's human resource information system, which often includes information on performance, participation in training and development programs, leadership potential, veteran status, gender, ethnicity, pay grade, and most recent merit increase and job change. The addition of nonsurvey performance data, whether customer satisfaction, sales performance, or attrition, can connect employees' opinions and their demographic details with important business outcomes. Linking those pieces together creates a rich database that can be queried to understand critical people issues.

If that sounds complicated, it doesn't have to be. Insightful analytics are mainly a result of hypothesis testing. This kind of analysis approaches the data with a specific question or assumption in mind, such as, "Employees' positive relationships with their managers will reduce voluntary attrition" or "Millennial employees value corporate philanthropy programs and the organization's commitment to a green workplace more than employees from the Baby Boomer generation." The analysis then focuses on testing that hypothesis, selecting the response data, demographics, and performance data necessary and then studying the patterns in the data.

However, many insights can also be based on happy accidents or discoveries. You might detect unusual data patterns, and your follow-up analysis reveals something previously unknown. Scans of the results show a blip that upon further investigation uncovers an at-risk population. Throwing all the data elements into the analytic mix and seeing what emerges can produce a surprising light bulb moment. This approach lets the analysis do all the work in uncovering insights.

Hypotheses and Happy Discoveries

So then, which is the right approach, hypothesis driven or relying on chance? They both are.

If business strategy, organization effectiveness, and success have inspired survey content and design, then the post-survey analytics are at least partly hypothesis driven. The data collected reflect what is most important to leaders and most related to future success. Subsequent analytics will reveal where the organization is progressing on these elements, and where it may be lagging. It will uncover the pockets of the organization that can serve as role models for other units, and provide insights into how various employee subgroups are reacting to changes in the organization. Analytics are focused on those subunits and employee groups that are viewed as most critical to the organization's success or most at risk.

A hypothesis-driven approach ensures from the outset that the necessary data elements are being captured. A study of whether the organization fosters a culture of inclusion, for example, can only happen if the organization asks the right questions in the survey, so the design of those questions may be inspired by previous research on the elements of an inclusive environment. As another example, let's say your organization wants to understand the impact of the adoption of Lean principles on organization effectiveness. That means the survey must capture data on the degree to which these behaviors have been adopted, and be able to identify which segments of the organization have been actively implementing Lean principles.

Recently, a client that was conducting a short quarterly survey of employees experienced a major corporate event when the company was acquired. The survey team was interested in seeing how the survey results changed as employees absorbed this news. They were disappointed, however, to see very little change in the results. Why? The survey questions focused on employees' day-to-day experiences, which were not affected by the acquisition. The survey didn't include questions about organization direction or strategy, or confidence in the future of the company or in senior leaders. Without the right questions, they weren't able to get the insights they were looking for. Critical hypotheses cannot be tested unless the necessary data have been collected.

Having said that, there is value in simply seeing what emerges from the data. This approach, sometimes called "dust bowl empiricism" by those in the social sciences, refers to findings and conclusions that are based on data patterns rather than driven by hypotheses or theory. In reality, survey data analysis is never fully done in the dust bowl, as survey content is influenced by the organization's data needs, known drivers of engagement, or both. Survey content is never random; there is nearly always a reason that certain questions are included in the survey. But sometimes you don't know what you don't know. Analyzing data based solely on established theories of organization effectiveness assumes everything is already known and little if anything remains to be discovered or understood. Times change, technologies change, people change, and organizations change, so it is logical to think that what you knew then may not work now. The dust bowl can be a valuable way to uncover those shifts.

A team I was working with was tasked with developing a union vulnerability indicator that could be embedded in surveys and would flag those company locations that were most at risk for unionization campaigns. One faction of the team insisted that the approach to this indicator should be driven by previous research and theory on the factors that lead to employee interest in union representation. A second faction favored the dust bowl approach.

Team Theory researched the literature on the topic and developed a set of questions and an algorithm that would be used to evaluate union vulnerability. Team Dust bowl used a large data set to determine which of more than 100 questions and demographics were most closely related to union membership, which was a data element in the database. The two approaches to developing the union vulnerability index were quite different, and not surprisingly they produced two very different indexes. Which worked the best? Team Dust bowl. When tested with client data, the dust bowl approach was more effective in accurately identifying hot spots in organizations.

Does this suggest that it is always best to ignore theory and just follow the data? Of course not. Much is known about organization effectiveness and the workplace factors that create engagement, and it would be a mistake to ignore that base of knowledge. Creating survey content without any sort of unifying framework will yield a hodgepodge of data that cannot provide meaningful insights. Theory, hypotheses, and random analysis all play a role in uncovering insight. It makes good sense to structure survey content and analysis based on what is most important to know now, but leave open the possibility that the organization doesn't know what it doesn't know.

A Data Analysis Primer

Data analysis can seem complicated and technical, and it can be. But when it comes to analyzing survey data, in general the simplest statistics are the most meaningful. Advanced analytics are not necessary to uncover critical insights. Percentages, trends from previous surveys, and differences calculated between demographic groups, external benchmarks, or leading and lagging groups can tell the tale quite effectively. So what is the best approach to analyzing survey results to yield data-driven insights?

Start at the Top of the Pyramid

A good way to start analyzing survey results is to approach the data initially at the total company level. What are the strengths and opportunities? What results are unexpected? Then, drill into the data based on these overall observations: Which subunits or demographic groups show lower or higher scores? Are there topics that are low relative to external benchmarks and are also declining from the previous survey? Drill further into the results using a combination of hierarchy groups and demographics. Investigate the nuances of scores across geographic regions. Go deeper into the data set to uncover insights.

It isn't necessary to do a complete and detailed assessment of every topic on the survey. Starting the analysis at the top of the data pyramid will identify those survey items and categories that have the greatest influence on employee engagement, for example, or provide a strategic insight into the effectiveness of the organization. Follow the trail of data that is most insightful to leaders.

Cross-tabulation reports are efficient, effective approaches to assessing the differences (or lack of differences) in the patterns of results for different employee groups. Cross-tabs are data tables that list survey questions or categories as the rows, and demographic groups as the columns. The cells of the table display the results for a specific group on a specific question or category. These tables make it relatively simple to scan survey data across demographics such as location, tenure group, and job type to find the outliers, or those subgroups that are substantially higher or lower than the rest. Heat maps are cross-tab tables where the cells of the table are color-coded to reflect score ranges (such as 90-100 percent favorable, 70-80 percent favorable, and so on) or statistically significant differences from the overall company. The colors illustrate the patterns in the data graphically.

Once you have identified key themes in the data, begin to uncover the factors that are influencers. Influencers may be external to the survey data, such as recent leadership changes, shifts in product mix, organization restructuring, or downsizing. Influencers may also be found within the data; driver analyses can uncover the influencers of a theme in the data. While most commonly used for determining the drivers of engagement, a driver analysis can be conducted on any survey question or category, and the results can be very insightful. For example, a jump in the percentage of employees who are considering leaving the organization may be explained through a driver analysis. Simple correlation coefficients can describe the relationships between survey questions and topics.

It is important to understand the similarities and differences for all employee groups, particularly those employee groups most central to organization success or most critical to the achievement of strategic objectives. A deep dive into the results for senior executives, research and development staff, salespeople, or other revenue generators, for example, can be used to inform actions that will have the greatest positive impact on the organization. Key talent groups may also include at-risk groups, meaning those that are at greatest risk of voluntarily leaving the company, or are most essential to diversity objectives or other key organizational initiatives.

It is also worth identifying the drivers of important metrics for key talent groups. Different employee groups are motivated by different sets of workplace elements, so it can be insightful to understand the nuances between them, rather than assuming all employees are engaged in the same manner.

Weave in External Context

Organizations never operate in a vacuum, and the interpretation of survey data almost always benefits from data or insights that originate from outside the survey data set. In the survey analysis world, context most often comes in the form of external benchmark data and a record of significant organization events and happenings. Significant shifts in survey results, either upward or downward, can be a function of organization changes ranging from new leadership; restructuring; the introduction of new programs, policies, and practices; fluctuations in the company's stock price; or the successful (or not so successful) launch of new products or services. These events represent influences on employee engagement or organization effectiveness that are unmeasured, or difficult to measure via survey questions. It is often very useful to create a timeline of meaningful changes in the organization in relation to the survey administration schedule to assist in interpreting the survey results.

A recent client of mine had a large percentage of employees working in its customer support organization. They spent their days on the phone with customers, resolving billing issues, responding to complaints, or scheduling visits for the technician team to install or repair equipment. A recent change in the terms and conditions of service contracts resulted in lower fees for new clients and was successful in attracting new business, but it infuriated the existing client base, many of whom had been paying much higher prices for many years. The customer support team bore the brunt of their dissatisfaction, and could do little to assist them. The company finally amended terms for existing customers, but not before the very negative situation took a significant toll on the customer support team, which was reflected in sharply lower survey results.

In this circumstance, it was very important to look at results for this population separate from the rest of the organization, because the introduction of new customer terms had a disparate negative impact on a specific group of employees. Analyzing the survey results without this context would have easily resulted in the misinterpretation of the survey data and the implementation of actions that would not have addressed the central issue.

External survey benchmarks or norms provide a perspective on what's typical when it comes to survey data. External benchmarks answer questions like, "Is 65 percent favorable a good score or something to worry about?" Not all survey questions are created equal in the sense that every question can achieve the same favorability levels. Some questions and topics typically receive high scores, and others receive low scores. A comparison with an external benchmark or reference point highlights where scores are within or outside the range of what's expected. Norms are particularly valuable when analyzing and interpreting global survey data, as cultural norms have a strong influence on survey results. Relying on an internal comparison across countries within the organization will lead to misunderstanding and misinterpretation, so survey data analysts are well advised to use external country or region norms to make sense of global data.

External benchmarks can be intoxicating for certain leaders, particularly those who are quantitatively inclined and motivated to exceed the average. These leaders can sometimes reduce the analysis of survey data to a race to exceed the benchmark, and focus their time and attention on understanding the gap between company results and the benchmark for key questions. They may request more and more specifically focused benchmarks, such as those based on organization performance, industry or subindustry, or combination of the two. Benchmarks are tools for interpretation and evaluation, but they should not be the sole focus of the survey or the analysis of the results. Beating the benchmark should not be the goal of the survey, and survey action plans should not be based on increasing scores to exceed the benchmark. Overuse of benchmarks in analysis and reporting of survey data distract leaders from focusing on key survey findings and nuanced action planning, as well as create bad habits in leaders.

Use Comment Data Strategically

Senior leaders are fond—and proud—of saying, "I read all the survey comments. Every single one." On the surface that claim sounds great; the leader is motivated to learn more about what is going on in the organization and has devoted a significant amount of their time to study the data in depth. Fair enough. The problem with this claim, however, is that reading thousands of comments, presented in no particular order and with no unifying framework, does little to drive insight. Without some way to organize and summarize the comments and their themes, what is best remembered by the reader are those comments that are compelling, emotional, and beautifully written, or those comments that fit neatly with the leader's preconceived ideas about what the issues are and what needs to be done about them.

Comments are valuable, to be sure, but they need to be themed and used in close cooperation with the quantitative survey data to provide maximum insight and impact. Once the major themes and issues have been identified through an analysis of the survey data, pull comments selectively to provide color and interpretive elements. Which comment themes inform the data patterns? Which subgroups of employees have the most to say about a topic? Some survey data analysis platforms allow comments to be filtered by responses to the survey questions, allowing a view of those comments written by employees who intend to leave the company, for example, or don't believe they have the tools and resources to do their jobs effectively.

When reviewing comment data, keep in mind that comments tend to have a negative bias. For many employees, writing a comment is their best or only chance to provide direct feedback to leaders, and most often that chance is used to share what needs to be changed or improved. What may be viewed as a preponderance of negative comments can alternatively be interpreted as constructive feedback from employees who want to see the company succeed.

Comments provide additional flavor and insight into issues uncovered in the survey and can be a valuable stepping-stone to creating effective actions. However, they can be overused in data analysis. Consider comments to be the salt and pepper on the lunch plate of survey data. Just as the right amount can enhance the taste of food, comments can provide the emotion, color, and detail to enhance understanding of survey results. But comments must be balanced with data in a way that illuminates survey data, making it come alive for the audience.

Link With Outcomes

Combining survey results with business performance data takes survey results from the realm of "employee issues" to that of "business issues." Leaders can see very clearly which workplace elements are driving attrition, customer satisfaction, or achievement of sales quotas, for example. One of the most common linkage analyses can help uncover the drivers of voluntary attrition. Survey results for those employees who voluntarily left the organization in the months after the survey can be compared with those employees who remained. This analysis can uncover unique drivers of attrition across key skill groups or businesses and ultimately provide the elements needed to develop predictive models of attrition.

As an example, an organization I worked with wanted to understand the factors influencing high levels of attrition, particularly among their key talent groups. The company was growing very quickly, but was struggling with holding on to top talent. Six months after the completion of the employee survey, the client sent us a file of all employees who had voluntarily left the organization. The file further specified which employees were "regretted" losses (high performers or high-potential employees) and which were "nonregretted" losses (generally those with performance issues). This file allowed us to add new demographics to the employees' survey record indicating whether they had left the organization, and if so, whether the departure was regretted or nonregretted.

The analysis that followed was relatively straightforward. We compared survey scores, both at the individual-question level and at the category level, of those employees who remained with the organization six months after the close of the survey and those who had left the organization. The largest gaps in the scores between those employees who left and those who remained provide insight into why an employee would choose to leave the organization. Our initial findings are detailed in Table 7-1.

It is no surprise that employee engagement was near the top of both lists; research has indicated that employee engagement is a significant influencer of willingness to stay with an organization.

Beyond that similarity, what is most interesting about these two groups is the differences in the pattern of results.

Table 7-1. Largest Category Score Gaps Between Employees Who Stayed and Left

Regretted Attrition	Nonregretted Attrition
1. Engagement	1. Innovation
2. Commitment	2. Engagement
3. Achievement	3. Immediate Manager
4. Innovation	4. Achievement
5. Execution	5. Recognition

The immediate manager category ranked third for nonregretted attrition, but didn't appear on the regretted attrition list. The largest differences between this group and remaining employees focused on commitment, achievement, innovation, and execution.

Table 7-2 shows the largest differences between the two attrition groups and remaining employees at the question level, providing more detailed evaluation for why top talent and high performers were leaving the company.

Table 7-2. Question Score Gaps in Regretted and Nonregretted Attrition

Regretted Attrition	Nonregretted Attrition
Career goals can be met	Manager values my opinion
Sense of accomplishment	Manager recognizes good work
Positives of working here make the effort worth it	Manager follows through
Time spent on work that challenges me	Manager is right a lot
Encouraged to find new and better ways	Manager seeks out diversity of thought
Involved in decisions	Manager inspires high performance
Like the work I do	Manager helps me adjust work plans
Have tools and resources to do my job	Manager coaches me on my career
My opinion is valued	

The results confirmed that employees considered regretted attrition left the organization for very different reasons than did those employees who were considered nonregretted attrition. A listing of the largest gaps in scores between those who stayed and those who left indicated that the regretted attrition employees were frustrated in their roles. They were not able to spend time on work that challenged them, they lacked the tools and resources they needed, and the effort required to get work done outweighed the benefits of working with the company. Consequently, they experienced less sense of accomplishment and liked their work less than those employees who remained. Not surprisingly, they were far less likely to believe their career goals could be met at the company. It was simply not worth it to work there.

On the other hand, note that every statement on the list of largest negative gaps for the nonregretted group includes the word *manager*. These statements appeared in different survey categories, but they all shared the common thread of the manager. This was not completely unexpected. Because many of these employees were considered performance issues, their managers were closely involved in overseeing their performance, and in most instances had imposed a performance improvement plan. The employees knew that their performance was a problem, and may have resented their managers' perceived overinvolvement in their day-to-day work experience.

This analysis, although simple, was very powerful. There is a common belief in organizations that employees "join companies, but leave managers." Our analysis used data to suggest that this was not the case for high-performing and high-potential employees, at least in this company. Largely, the employees who seemed to leave managers were the ones the company did not mind losing. In contrast, the work environment and being enabled to get work accomplished was the primary factor that drove top performers out of the company. Their relationship with their manager was less of a factor in their decision to leave the company. Without these data, the organization may have taken action based on the myth and not the fact. They may have invested heavily in shoring up manager skills, and while generally this isn't a bad investment, it would not have solved this problem. Data revealed what was necessary to address the loss of top talent in the organization.

A Look Inside Survey Data: Common Patterns

Organizations are complex and nuanced. Most operate across multiple locations, some with employees in different countries. They support a variety of products for many types of customers. The average organization has employees working in dozens of job families, at many different organizational levels, and with enormous variability in their years of service, ethnic background, and pay grade, to name just a few potential differentiators. Some are first-line supervisors, others are managers of managers, some are individual contributors, and others make decisions that have the power to change the direction and fortunes of the company.

It is fair to say that great diversity in the employee population yields great diversity in employee experiences and opinions. Thorough understanding of survey data requires understanding the nuances in survey results across all employee types and experiences. Assuming that a diverse set of employees shares a common perspective on the organization can result in drawing conclusions that do not reflect any particular employee group, and creating generic action plans that do not address the needs of most employees. Implementing such actions is a poor investment of the organization's resources, and the limited positive result stemming from these actions will do little to build the reputation of the organization's survey as a tool for organizational change and improvement.

Years of research have identified common patterns in survey responses. Understanding these patterns sharpens interpretation of survey data because you'll know which to anticipate and avoid over-interpreting. Recognizing when the organization's results conform or, more tellingly, don't conform to expected patterns in the data focuses analysis on the most insightful findings—the ones that hook the attention of leaders and drive meaningful actions. The most predictable patterns in survey data fall into a handful of categories.

Years of Service

New hires are always more engaged and favorable on virtually every survey question than longer-serving employees. This pattern is commonly called the honeymoon effect. New employees have just completed a courtship with the company. They met, got to know each other, and then decided to enter into a relationship. Things are always great at the beginning of a new relationship, and a new employment relationship is no exception. The company is inspiring, learning a new role is exciting, and your co-workers are congenial.

The duration of the honeymoon effect varies by company, although in general the spell has worn off by about one year of service. Organizations that do a great deal of hiring for jobs that turn over rapidly, such as in a retail or customer call center environment, may find that the honeymoon is over sooner, and organizations that hire less often and have less turnover can expect the honeymoon to linger a bit longer.

What happens when the honeymoon effect wears off? Favorable scores for employee engagement and other survey topics drop off dramatically after the first six to 12 months, and then typically continue to decline through midcareer, although at a lesser rate. The timing of midcareer can vary across companies. It could be eight to 10 years of service at companies where long-term service is the norm, or three to five years at organizations that see greater turnover and therefore have a smaller percentage of long-serving employees.

After midcareer, one of two patterns tends to emerge. One pattern shows a slight and gradual improvement in most survey topics through the top end of employee service, although scores never reach the levels attained in the first year. This pattern produces a trend line that looks a bit like a fishhook, starting high in early years, dropping sharply, bottoming, then recovering slightly (Figure 7-1). The second pattern more closely resembles a hockey stick. Results bottom out in midcareer and stay at that level through the top end of employee service levels. There is no discernable improvement.

There are some variations, of course. While most survey categories will decline predictably, some, like feelings about pay or benefits, may improve with more years of service, as longer service often yields higher pay. Other categories may continue their decline, not recovering when a bottom has been achieved. A good example of this is opportunities for advancement. Not surprisingly, longer-serving employees may see fewer opportunities for career movement and growth than employees with less service.

Figure 7-1. Survey Results by Length of Service

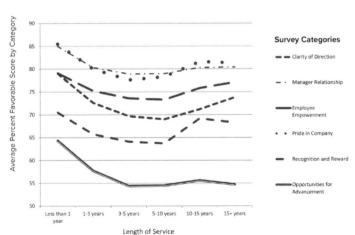

Source: Johnson and Mastrangelo (2008)

Locale

It is no surprise to anyone who has traveled abroad or done business globally that there are clear differences in country cultures. Some cultures are more deferential to authority. Others are relatively informal when it comes to relationships between managers and employees. Some cultures encourage long workdays, while others have limits on the number of hours in a day that employees are allowed to work and provide generous vacation and leave benefits. Some cultures are welcoming to working women, others much less so.

These recognizable cultural differences translate into common patterns of survey responses (Figure 7-2). Survey scores in Japan may seem shockingly low in comparison with other countries. Conversely, survey results in Latin American countries are remarkably favorable. This pattern should not be interpreted to mean that leaders and managers in Latin America are doing a much better job engaging employees than their counterparts in Japan. The difference in results reflects the unique cultures and response patterns of these parts of the world. Employees in emerging economies, such as parts of Eastern Europe, tend to respond more favorably to survey questions than employees in more developed and mature economies, such as Western Europe and the United States. And speaking of the United States, Americans are generally less favorable than their colleagues in Latin America, but more favorable than those in Europe.

Research on this topic, including Geert Hofstede's seminal model of cultural dimensions, has identified common patterns and the specific cultural norms that account for the differences (Hofstede 1984). External benchmark data by country or region is very helpful in interpreting country data. For example, viewing the company's data from employees in Japan in the context of an external Japanese benchmark resets conclusions from panic over low scores to relief that the low score is not a concern. The scores could even be a good thing if they exceed the benchmark for Japan.

Figure 7-2. Sample Survey Results Around the World

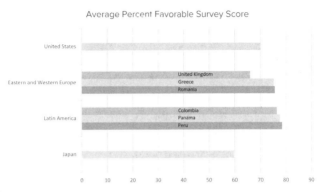

Average Percent Favorable Survey Score

Industry

Manufacturing organizations operate very differently from financial services organizations, which operate very differently from retail organizations. Given that, it seems logical that survey scores would have different patterns across industries. However, there is little variation in scores (Figure 7-3).

Figure 7-3. Survey Scores Show Minimal Variability Across Industries

Survey Category	Financial	Healthcare	Consumer Goods	Consumer Services	Oil and Gas	Industrial	Technology
Clarity of Direction	74.8	76.2	73.8	70.9	72.8	69.3	72.5
Manager Relationship	83	78.8	79.7	81.4	80.7	77.6	78.8
Performance Management	78.5	78.1	79.8	78.3	76.1	77.8	78.2
Employee Empowerment	75.1	75.9	73.4	72.7	71	72.4	69.8
Pride in Company	82.9	81	82.2	80.1	80.6	78.1	76.1
Continuous Improvement	65.3	67.9	64.9	62.7	70.2	62.4	58.2
Teamwork and Collaboration	74.6	75.2	74	69.8	68	64.2	67.2
Recognition and Reward	66.4	65.5	67	63.1	58.9	60.2	63.6
Resources and Support	74.2	74.8	70	71.1	72.4	71.3	64.2
Learning and Development	77.1	75.4	73.1	72.6	68.8	68.2	70.1
Opportunities for Advancement	59.6	59.7	54.8	52.3	60.4	52.3	56.9
Average Score	75.47	75.18	73.72	72.27	72.22	70.50	70.01

Source: Perceptyx Survey Benchmarking Database

100% - 80%
79% - 60%
59% - 40%

Any organization comprises a wide variety of employees, from hourly workers to professionals, from sales clerks to research scientists. Regardless of industry, it has employees performing jobs that are routine and low level, or jobs that are expertise driven and involve innovation and self-direction. Different industries have different ratios of lower-level and higher-level roles. Because survey scores tend to be lowest in lower-level roles and highest in higher-level roles, different ratios yield different overall scores.

Organization Level

It should come as no surprise that a day in the life of a senior executive is very different from that of a production employee, or a salesperson or a customer call center representative. The obvious differences include hours worked and physical workspace. More subtle differences include access to communications and knowledge of the strategic direction of the organization. Different roles in the organization, whether defined by skill group or level in the organization's hierarchy, are associated with different career options and trajectories, opportunities for learning and development, and reward structures. In short, there are significant differences in the experiences of an organization's employees, even though they share an employer.

These differences in work experience yield different patterns in survey scores. In general, the higher the employee group sits in the organization pyramid, the more favorable their survey results will be (Figure 7-4). Senior leaders tend to be more positive on just about every survey question and category than all other employee groups. Leaders have access to important information and insights about the organization. Most have the tools, resources, and support they need to do their work, and their roles have a significant impact on the organization. They are closely involved in making decisions that propel the organization forward, and they are well compensated for the work that they do. The work experience is quite different at all the levels below leadership.

Figure 7-4. Survey Scores Are Highest at the Top of the Organizational Hierarchy

Survey Category	Executive	Manager	Individual Contributor
Manager Relationship	87.5	84.1	79.8
Pride in Company	87	82.5	79.5
Clarity of Direction	83.8	76.1	72.1
Employee Empowerment	83.8	80.2	74.6
Performance Management	83	80.5	78.1
Learning and Development	80	74.4	71.3
Recognition and Reward	78.1	69.8	64.7
Resources and Support	77.4	73.9	73.3
Teamwork and Collaboration	76.3	72.7	68.5
Continuous Improvement	73.6	69.1	62.9
Opportunities for Advancement	67	61	56.1

Source: Perceptyx Survey Benchmarking Database

100% - 80%
79% - 60%
59% - 40%

It is a significant finding indeed when scores for senior leaders dip below those for roles at lower levels in the hierarchy. This can suggest a crisis in confidence in the organization, a breakdown in communications between top executives and lower levels of leadership, or senior executives who are out of touch with the current reality of the organization. In any case, additional analysis is required to further understand the issues.

It is an equally significant finding when results for senior leaders far exceed those for the levels of the organization below them. Of course we expect to see some differences, but when these differences are excessive, that indicates executives have lost touch with the rest of the organization. Larger-than-average gaps in scores around confidence in the future of the organization, understanding of strategy, and even engagement suggest that leaders have become detached from the general population. This isn't always an easy discussion to have with leaders; a typical reaction may be that "they just don't get it."

We should expect leaders to have a different perspective on the organization than the rest of the employee base. Leaders should be highly engaged, confident, and keenly aware of the strategy and direction of the organization. But the best leaders have a clear view of life outside the executive suite, and remain close to the daily work experience of their staff, all the way down to the shop floor. They are able to understand life in the organization from not only their point of view but also that of other significant employee groups. They recognize that not every employee sees the opportunities or challenges they see, and they take action to address the discrepancies.

Survey results are an invaluable tool for leaders to gain that perspective. Presenting these cuts of data to leaders expands their understanding of what is going on throughout the organization, and how to act in a way that is specific to the needs of different employee groups. True insight from survey data is a product of careful analysis and interpretation. As such, it is important to know what to look for in the data:

- Recognize the common patterns in survey data, whether by tenure, position in the organization, or region of the world. Without this understanding, survey results can be easily misinterpreted or overinterpreted, leading to action plans that do not reflect real issues in the organization.
- External benchmarks can provide valuable context in understanding what is typical when it comes to survey data patterns. Using benchmark data judiciously helps to identify which data fluctuations are to be expected, and which represent strengths or opportunity areas for the organization.
- The typical patterns in survey data reflect commonality in the work experiences of various employee groups. Be realistic in expectations for results in different work environments, and plan actions and goals accordingly.

Awareness of the expected patterns in survey data allows survey data analysis to proceed efficiently, letting survey users sort expected differences in results from true insights.

Building Your HR Analytics Engine

Effective analysis of survey data need not be complicated, but it should be done with the intent to understand organization issues and respond to leader questions with a quantitative, fact-based approach. To use the organization's survey as an HR analytics engine:

- Develop content that reflects the issues of greatest value to the organization, both strategically and tactically. Asking the right questions leads to collecting the data needed to study critical issues. A well-designed survey strategy will yield a plan that collects the right data at the right time.

- Incorporate as much data as possible. True insight comes from analyses that understand the nuances in the results, and pinpoint where issues are more significant and in need of action.

- Linking survey data to business metrics underscores the importance of the insights to the success of the business.

- Start small; HR analytics does not have to be complex to provide valuable insights and inspire action. Many analytics projects can be completed using survey supplier software and tools, as long as the necessary data elements are there.

Organization surveys can produce vast amounts of data and information, but well-thought-out and careful analysis of survey data yields insight. The story of the data emerges through determining which findings are typical and which are unique, what has changed over time, and what has remained the same. When reviewing survey results with senior leaders, there is nearly always the question "Why?" Why are we seeing this pattern? Why have scores changed? Why is a particular group responding in this fashion? Analytics provide the answers.

8

A CONSULTANT MINDSET AND YOUR SURVEY STRATEGY

Organizations are complex, comprising a variety of functions, skill groups, locations, leadership styles, business units, and markets. Programs and actions that make sense in one part of the organization may be ineffective in another; there is no plan that will be equally effective in every corner of the organization. So when it comes to using survey data, what is the best way to provide tailored analyses and approaches for action?

Using survey data effectively across subunits in an organization requires the assistance of HR business partners. These individuals are embedded within the organization's subunits, and understand the business challenges, structure, and players involved, from leaders to managers to individual contributors. HR business partners are the members of the extended survey team who can best interpret the survey results in the current context of the organization. Additionally, they can partner with managers and leaders to use the findings to create action that drives important changes within subunits.

What Role Should HR Play?

HR professionals need an increasingly wide range of skills to be a business partner. They must understand workforce demographics, global culture, business strategy, and leaders' priorities against the backdrop of customer, market, and financial results. They need to operate as internal consultants, taking on multiple roles in the business and leveraging a variety of capabilities. The role continuum shown in Figure 8-1 demonstrates the different roles HR professionals may take on. These roles are a function of the individual HR professional's skills, the needs of the business and its leaders, and the situation in which the HR professional finds themselves.

Figure 8-1. The Role Continuum for HR Professionals

To some extent, each of these roles is necessary to successfully support a business unit during the survey planning, administration, and analysis process. The tactician role is critical during survey planning, because often the core survey team will invite HR business partners to participate as members of an extended team of survey advisers. In this tactical role, the HR business partners ensure that the organization hierarchy is represented accurately, determine what additional steps or resources are required for successful survey administration, and work with managers and leaders to make sure that data reports are accurately distributed and any survey data analysis and action planning-training is delivered. This is a necessary role for successful survey administration, but not one that will enable strategic use of survey data.

Generalists take the relationship with leaders and managers a bit further, supplementing tactical skills with a greater depth of knowledge of HR issues in the organization and greater focus on HR content, programs, and practices. HR business partners with a generalist role are informative and attentive, but reactive, providing information to the business, primarily when leaders request it.

HR business partners with more advanced skills can take on the role of coach or adviser, proactively providing insights to leaders about their leadership styles and encouraging them to initiate necessary programs and practices. The business partner in this role suggests solutions to leaders based on an assessment of data and anecdotal evidence, both current and future looking, encouraging them to take actions that will enhance the functioning and success of the business.

Each of these three roles—tactician, generalist, and coach or adviser—can play an important part in use of the survey data. From validating the accuracy of data reporting to summarizing results to providing basic data interpretation and action plans, HR professionals play a critical role in ensuring that the organization's survey informs leadership on key issues. They also help implement the actions that will enhance the organization and communicate to employees that their voices made a difference to the business. But there is a more advanced role that HR business partners can take on, one with the power to transform the survey process into an intelligence-gathering exercise.

HR business partners who take on the role of consultant anticipate the needs of the organization and how survey data can provide the insights necessary to move forward strategically. Consultants take a systems view of the organization, recognizing the marketplace, resource, and strategic challenges of the subunit, but also understand its leadership dynamics, staffing and talent issues, and culture. Consultants appreciate the multiple components of the organization as well as the internal and external demands on the organization. They go beyond advising senior leaders on important issues to uncovering data and insights that the organization wouldn't have found on its own. They provide business intelligence and influence not just post-survey actions, but the direction of the business unit. They see the survey as more than feedback on employee engagement and its drivers. They use survey results to uncover critical workforce issues via analytics and a deep understanding of the organization, its leaders, and its challenges.

What are the skills needed to be an effective consultant to senior leaders? Consider the six skills identified by Dave Ulrich and colleagues (2012) and how they relate to the organizational survey:

1. **Credible Activist:** Establishes personal trust with leaders via business acumen. Actively works to build relationships, delivers on promises, and communicates clearly and consistently with integrity. Demonstrates not just subject matter expertise, but clear understanding of the business and a commitment to making the business successful. Understands how the survey results links to business metrics and goals.

2. **HR Innovator and Integrator:** Knows and applies current trends for human capital and talent practices. Converts and implements HR practice areas into organizational

solutions. Uses survey results to assess emerging HR trends and challenges in the business.

3. **Technology Proponent:** Uses technology solutions, including survey reporting and analytics platforms, to deliver HR administrative functions, in this case analysis and interpretation of survey data. Uses technology to improve communication and networking, as well as to enhance information, relationships, and efficiency.

4. **Strategic Positioner:** Thinks and acts from the outside in, translating business trends, insights based on a keen understanding of the external marketplace, and employee survey data into internal decisions and actions. Identifies client segments and aligns organization actions to client needs.

5. **Capability Builder:** Defines and builds organizational capabilities required to deliver on strategy, both in the leadership and individual contributor populations. Works to institutionalize capabilities that define unique culture, processes, and identities of the organization. Assesses current organizational culture via survey data and analytics.

6. **Change Champion:** Integrates organizational changes, sustains disciplined change processes, initiates change, and works to overcome resistance to change. Uses survey data to build the case for change.

How HR Can Use Surveys to Become a Business Partner

It is far too easy for leaders and managers to focus on the numbers aspect of survey results, and many default to simply tracking changes in scores from previous surveys and evaluating their results against internal or external benchmarks. And while there is nothing inherently wrong with this approach, as a default use of survey results it fails to provide true insight that drives the business, and does not encourage leaders to think about the survey as a source of business intelligence.

To truly drive change and improvements in the organization, HR professionals need to become consultants and engagement coaches for their organizations. They must guide them through an insightful analysis of the data, take advantage of survey reporting technology, incorporate nonsurvey performance metrics, and propose changes and actions that are for the good of the business, not just for the next round of survey scores.

While most HR professionals are familiar with the types of data and reports standard to the survey process, they might not be equipped to consult with leaders and managers when it comes to using survey results strategically in the business. In most cases, it is necessary to establish this as an expectation for the HR business partner team, and to develop these capabilities through some sort of training or workshop.

It helps to think of survey results as a hierarchy of impact (Figure 8-2). Survey results provide a significant amount of data, from overall scores on individual questions and categories to demographic cross-tabs, change from previous surveys, and internal and external benchmark comparisons.

Data form the foundation of understanding, and the multiple data elements from the survey are the critical inputs to information, which identifies challenges and opportunities, improvements and declines. Information provides a description of the organization at the time of the survey, and it informs leaders and managers about the current strengths and weaknesses of the organization. A lot of data are often required to produce information in an easily consumable format.

Information is essential, but insight is what drives meaningful change and improvements in the organization. It takes business context into account, both internal and external to the organization, as well as an appreciation of how the business and the external market may change in the future. Insight is driven by an understanding of the organization's critical subsets—whether skill groups, lines of business, or demographic groups—and a hypothesis-driven approach to data analysis to uncover the unique results for each group. Insight guides a recognition that a single set of actions applied across the entire organization will likely not produce the results desired. However, unique actions targeted to specific groups that are key to success will carry the organization forward successfully. Insights are focused, specific, and, when well done, often limited to a very short but meaningful list.

Figure 8-2. Hierarchy of Impact

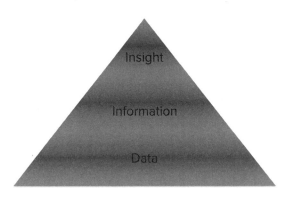

Interpreting Survey Results

Analyzing and interpreting survey data to provide true insight can be accomplished by going beyond the data published in manager reports to incorporate context and an assessment of the impact of actions on the organization. Figure 8-3 provides a simple tool and process to support the transition from data to information to insight.

Figure 8-3. Sample Results Interpretation Tool

Use this planning tool to review data and results, prioritize areas with the greatest strengths and potential opportunities, and offer solutions to address the priority themes for your client, function, or enterprise. Complete each section to prepare for client discussions.

Client Name:

Review Results	Define Themes	Refine Impact	Propose Action
• Utilize the reporting platform to explore data and list key findings: » managers' toolkit » participation (respond/ complete) » favorability (category and item) » comment (frequency and topic) » comparison (relevant segments) » reference (demographics).	• Synthesize key findings into themes that combine individual item or category data into usable, related information. • Consider relevant business and functional factors that may be relevant areas to investigate.	• Narrow down or refine the themes to include information and offer insights into causes and effects that exist within and among information. • Define possible risks, consequences, or benefits of addressing items.	• Offer solutions that address one or more themes or insights across an enterprise or within a function. • Suggest action that mitigates risks, takes advantage of inherent strengths, or improves performance and productivity.

1. **Review Results:** Utilize the reporting platform to explore the data and list the key findings, such as:
   ◦ Participation rates. Very low and very high rates of participation, not to mention large changes upward or downward from the previous survey, tell a story.
   ◦ Favorability scores, by both categories and questions. Understand that not all survey questions and categories will get high scores; what are the strengths of the organization, where is there room for improvement?
   ◦ Comment topics and frequency, and a link between responses to specific multiple-choice survey questions and comment themes.
   ◦ Comparisons of survey results to relevant groups, both internal and external to the organization. Where does the organization lead or lag other internal groups or external benchmarks?
   ◦ Differences between demographic and organizational groups. Do the demographic patterns of data match expectations, or are results an anomaly? Are critical skills groups favorable?

2. **Define Themes:** Synthesize the key findings into themes that combine individual item or category data into usable, related information. Consider relevant business and functional factors that may be relevant areas to investigate. Build a story with the survey data that weaves together multiple data points, employee groups, and critical internal and external context.

3. **Refine Impact:** Narrow down or refine the themes to identify the greatest potential for action. Include not only the description of the theme but also insights into causes and effects. Define possible risks, consequences, and benefits of acting or not acting to address issues. Why is

it critical to act, and what may happen if the organization fails to do so? Why is this finding essential to the success of the organization?

4. **Propose Actions:** Offer solutions that address one or more themes or insights across the enterprise or within a function. Suggest action that mitigates risks, takes advantage of inherent strengths, or improves performance and productivity. Whenever possible, look for opportunities to incorporate actions into ongoing programs or initiatives. Make the connection between the actions and the success of the business. This is not just an "HR thing," but a critical tactic that moves the organization closer to its vision of success.

How Do You Need to Report Data?

The unique nature of organizations extends to another step in the survey process: data reporting and employee feedback. The right format and procedures for sharing survey data with leaders and managers and providing insights to employees will vary from company to company. It is important to understand the capabilities of managers: How fluent are they with data? How comfortable do they feel with the topics included in the survey and with leading an employee feedback meeting? Can they reasonably be expected to influence the survey topics? Which levels of leadership are in the best position to make an impact on the issues raised in the survey?

Many survey providers have standard survey reporting formats, and generally can accommodate customization. Consider the behaviors that will be most beneficial to addressing survey issues in the short term, and to the organization in the long term. If the goal is to encourage managers to quickly interpret results, meet with their team, and put appropriate actions in place, it would be a mistake to inundate them with multiple data cuts and analyses. On the other hand, if the report user needs to dive deeply into a complex issue or organization, then they need a more detailed report. Match the report design with the report user.

The Importance of a Consultant Mindset

Consulting is really all about teaching and influencing. HR business partners who take on the role of consultant can teach leaders about the importance of people and people issues in their organization and demonstrate the value of data in making the best possible decisions about people. They can then influence the direction and success of the business through not just the implementation of critical actions inspired by survey insights, but by shaping the thinking of senior leaders about the role of talent in their organization.

Consulting conversations need to incorporate a number of fundamental actions to be successful and build an ongoing, trusting consultative relationship with leaders:

- **Ask and understand:** What are the goals of the organization? What do leaders want to accomplish? What are their beliefs about talent in their organization and their level of understanding of employee motivation, engagement, and the power of HR analytics?
- **Deepen and broaden perceptions:** This represents a teaching moment, when HR business partners can share lessons learned and case studies from other organizations, as well as research that demonstrates the link between engagement and business success.
- **Offer selective experience and expertise:** HR business partners should share their experiences in other business units or organizations. What worked best? What parallels are there between this organization and others? What can HR business partners offer to leaders in the way of unique perspectives and experiences that supplement those of the senior leadership team?

- **Support and guide the path forward:** The best recommendations a consultant partner can make are those that support the vision and direction of the business. Which insights can clarify the challenges ahead, and which actions can be implemented that can clear the path and help achieve the organization's objectives? HR business partners need to demonstrate their willingness to lead actions in their area of expertise and guide leaders through actions that may feel unfamiliar or challenging.
- **Acknowledge commitment:** Leaders want the organization to succeed, and while they may not be highly skilled in recognizing and acting upon people issues, it is critical to acknowledge their willingness to understand and act upon organization survey recommendations.
- **Recognize and cheer:** The work is not always easy, and results may take time. Encourage leaders to maintain their efforts, and recognize them for their attention to these issues.
- **Compliment and complement:** Leadership teams comprise individuals representing different areas of expertise, as well as different perspectives and experiences. The HR business partners' unique view of the organization and focus on talent complements the rest of the team's capabilities, and when provided in a timely and meaningful way can make a significant difference in the organization's success.

Organization survey results affect the organization at many levels. HR business partners have the relationships and capabilities to drive survey findings and actions deep in the organization, building upon their already established relationships and capabilities. Successful change requires the actions of many, so share the load across many hands in the organization.

9

PREPARE YOUR
ORGANIZATION
TO ACT

Conducting an organizational survey is a multistep process that unfolds over many months. Ideally the process kicks off with strategy development, followed by survey content design. During the survey administration phase, employees' responses are compiled and the database of results created. The analysis phase begins after data collection is complete, and focuses on interpreting survey results and outlining the findings. The final stage, reporting and taking action, involves preparing and distributing data reports to leaders throughout the organization. Distribution provides the opportunity to spread insights throughout the organization and invite action. Survey data can be a powerful catalyst for change and improvement in organizations.

However, taking advantage of this opportunity is often easier said than done. The post-survey action-planning process is where many survey programs break down and fail to deliver on their potential to drive meaningful change. There are several reasons why this phase of the process is problematic for organizations.

From Centralized Control to Distributed Responsibility

A centralized team generally manages the administration of the organization survey process, often in the organization's headquarters. This team is responsible for the strategy development, design, implementation, analysis, and reporting of results throughout the organization. It is often the liaison to a partner professional services firm that provides support and online tools for the survey process. The team makes the decisions, owns the activities, and leads the implementation of the process—that is, until reports are distributed to managers and the action-planning process begins.

Once reports are in managers' hands, the core team no longer controls the process. It may have designed the action-planning phase of the survey process, but the implementation is now distributed, meaning that hundreds, if not thousands, of individuals are responsible for what happens next. The core team needs to rely on this dispersed population to make the final phase of the project a success. Managers have their own perspective on and interest in the survey, and it is impossible to ensure that all will complete every task given to them, doing all they are told to do in the manner expected of them and according to a specified timeline. Many managers will complete all tasks given to them, many will complete some, others will use their own approach, and some will do nothing. The point is, the core team is not in charge of what happens next. Managers are. There are three primary reasons why leaders are reluctant to fully participate in survey feedback and action planning.

Managers Don't See the Connection

An overemphasis on the process can make survey data analysis and action planning feel like just one more task managers must complete on top of regular duties. The survey's content may not reflect the topics of greatest interest or value to managers, and consequently the results won't provide useful insights for enhancing the team's or the manager's performance. In this case, managers will fail to see the survey as a tool to enable their team's—and therefore their own—success, but rather something that HR has imposed upon them as part of the HR agenda.

A Lack of Capability

Interpreting survey data, providing survey feedback to employees, and creating action plans based on survey data require certain skills and capabilities. Surveys provide information and insight that may not be familiar to all managers, and they may feel uncomfortable discussing some of the topics with their team. Leading the discussion, seeking feedback, prioritizing issues, and determining which actions will have the most positive impact on the issues may seem foreign to many managers, and they may struggle to do the work well. Managers may be asked to use survey data and plan actions only once each year or even less, which can lead to acquired capabilities getting rusty, because they do not practice them frequently. Ultimately, the request made of them may feel so far out of their comfort zone that some avoid the process altogether and disregard the survey results.

The Action-Planning Process Is Too Complicated

To provide structure and accountability intended to control a widely distributed process, many organizations create an action-planning process that is complex and cumbersome. Action-planning tools and processes are often so complicated and time consuming that managers do not know where to start and may give up before they even get started. They believe too much is being asked of them, with little chance of a positive return on their time investment.

Any of these challenges can derail the action-planning process before it ever gets started. In that case, why bother? If organizations are serious about driving actions post-survey, the action-planning process must be simple, meaningful, and excuse-proof.

What Is Made Easy Gets Done

The phrase *what gets measured gets done* is used often in the business world. There is a good deal of truth in the statement, but when it comes to surveys, I would amend it to say, "What is made easy gets done." One of the primary reasons that actions do not get planned or implemented is that the action-planning process has become overengineered. I have seen all kinds of convoluted processes for action planning. Most of these design elements were well intentioned, but when HR professionals and survey administrators require reviews and approvals, verifications, or pass-throughs of issues to other managers or staff, or when they penalize managers who have not participated or do not participate correctly, they have not done anything to encourage the behaviors they want to see in the company. They ask a lot of managers, who have a lot on their plates. If HR professionals make the process difficult, they discourage managers from following through. Create an action-planning process that is easy to use and actually encourages managers to plan and implement actions, rather than discouraging them from participating. The specific details of the action-planning process—or even the action plan itself—are not what's important. You only need the plan as a precursor or catalyst to action; make it easy to plan the action so leaders can very quickly implement it.

Many managers are uncomfortable with survey data. They struggle to interpret the results and are unsure of how they should act. They can become defensive if they believe employees are criticizing them, when in fact employees are simply voicing their frustration with the broader work environment. If we want managers and the action-planning process to be successful, we cannot assume managers will know what to do and how to do it. We need to support them with resources, tools, and guidance. We need to eliminate the excuses managers may have to avoid using the results to act.

We want to set managers up for success, and we want employees to see that their input did make a difference to the organization. If we want the survey to be seen as an effective tool for improvement, we have to create an action-planning process that supports change.

What could be easier than a 1-2-3 approach to action planning? Identify one issue. Do two things about it, and discuss it with the team three times. It's easy to understand, and easy to implement.

The 1-2-3 Approach to Survey Action Planning

Why stop at one action when survey results can identify many issues that would benefit from action planning? The more action plans that managers create, the less likely they are to fully implement any of them. It almost doesn't matter which issue a manager picks; doing something is better than doing nothing, and you want to eliminate the anxiety many managers experience trying to choose the most important thing to work on. The proof point of the survey process for employees—what will encourage them to participate fully survey after survey and believe that leaders are truly listening—is that something happens as a result of their feedback. Managers need to act on something, be it low-hanging fruit or a more complex issue.

The 1-2-3 methodology may be simple, but managers still need resources, tools, and support to succeed. Make it foolproof to determine which actions make sense for a given issue. Most survey consulting firms provide an action-planning component as part of their suite of survey tools; in general, these tools provide an easy transition from survey reporting to action planning in a single user interface, and the seamlessness of the tools can facilitate taking action.

On the other hand, your company may already have internal tools for performance-goal setting or planning business objectives. If it has such tools and managers use them, they are a good option. This will help managers make the connection between using survey results to inform ongoing business decisions and plans.

In truth, there is no magic to a specific action-planning tool, so use the ones that make it easiest for managers to act on the survey results. Action-planning tools and templates, whether internal or provided by a vendor partner, must be intuitive. Give managers easy access to simple and helpful suggestions for action that are specific to the questions and themes in the survey tool. The objective is to create a process that is as foolproof and excuse-proof as possible. Figure 9-1 shows how simple an action-planning tool can be.

Figure 9-1. A Simple Action-Planning Tool

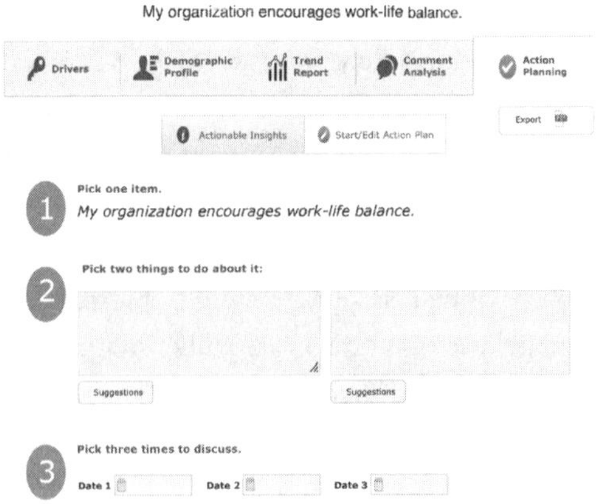

Tailor Action Planning to Managers' Capabilities

It would be a mistake to design and implement a survey process that is beyond the current capability of managers and leaders. When designing the survey strategy, be honest about what can be expected of managers and realistic about how they are able to participate. If the management team doesn't have the capability to understand and act on the topics covered in the organization's survey, the survey will not drive change and employees will come to believe that their feedback does not matter.

In many companies, it is necessary to take a crawl-walk-run approach when designing the survey strategy, meaning the early years of the survey program emphasize simplicity and building manager skills and capabilities. The topics covered in the survey should be straightforward, the data reports sent to managers need to be simple and easy to use, and the task to discuss results with employees and plan actions needs to be heavily scripted.

Some companies elect in the early years of their survey program to report results at relatively high levels of the company hierarchy and gradually move reporting and action-planning responsibility down throughout the organization as the process becomes more ingrained and managers build capability. Over time, the survey process can become more involved, incorporating more topics in the survey and moving more data interpretation and action-planning tasks to managers.

Interpreting survey results and planning and implementing actions can intimidate managers. The action-planning process must provide tools that enable managers to succeed. Provide questions to consider that will help managers think through workplace issues identified in the survey (Figure 9-2). Such questioning tools help the manager problem solve and think more comprehensively about employees' input. Include links to materials and resources that enable managers to expand their thinking on a topic.

Figure 9-2. Accessible Resources to Guide Managers to Action

Many organizations also build in links to their internal learning management system, which provides managers with access to additional readings or training. Suggested actions provide managers with examples of how to address issues uncovered in the survey. These actions should be clear, easy to implement, and likely to drive change.

Note that by providing managers with suggested actions, you're not doing their job for them; rather, you're nudging them in the right direction. Managers can certainly implement suggested actions as they are written, but they should also be encouraged to edit the suggested actions or write their own. The suggestions are a starting point, a guide to help them understand what a reasonable action to address an issue looks like.

Organizations will maximize the success of their employee survey program if they match the expectations of managers and leaders to their current thinking and capability. The ultimate objective is to help managers succeed, to not only get the plan created and implemented quickly, but also develop new people-leadership capabilities. The survey and action-planning process can be a great way for managers to develop skills such as listening and responding to employee input, working with data, prioritizing actions, and following through on commitments.

Managers who believe they have been set up to succeed are more likely to implement actions post-survey. When action plans are fully implemented and both managers and employees experience the positive changes that can result, the organization survey process becomes a valued tool for feedback, listening, and change.

Here are some final thoughts to make action planning excuse-proof and increase the likelihood that leaders and managers will act:

- Create survey content that is actionable at multiple levels of the organization. Give each level of management insights into issues over which they have control. Taking action at multiple levels of the organization increases the speed of change, but only if leaders and managers are given issues they can personally affect.

- Harness the momentum of survey administration to create anticipation of survey results and interest in action planning. The longer the time between when the data are collected and when results are distributed, the more likely action planning will be postponed or never happen at all. Managers are not compelled to act on data that they believe are old. It is important to move quickly.

- Meet managers where they are. Honestly evaluate their level of capability to use survey data and drive actions. Imposing a process that is beyond managers' abilities will frustrate them, not challenge them.

- Streamline the action-planning process with tools that are simple to understand, easy to use, and accessible. Repurpose existing goal- and performance-planning processes if they are well understood and frequently used. The objective is to create a sense of ease and comfort with tools.
- It is a mistake to assume that managers will know what issues are most in need of attention and which actions should be taken. Build nudges into data reports and the action-planning process that gently direct them toward critical topics and suggestions for improvements.

If the objective of survey action planning is to drive the success of the organization at all levels, then we need to ensure that managers can be successful in their use of survey data. Managers have a lot on their plate, and the HR organization shares the responsibility for much of what is on managers' to-do lists.

Between performance management, coaching, training and development, and compensation planning, managers may feel that they spend the bulk of their workweek on HR tasks. The challenge is to help managers see that the survey—and more important, taking action based on survey results—is not just another HR task, but rather an opportunity to enhance the functioning of their team or organization. Managers will engage with the process when they can see how taking action on survey results will improve the performance and success of their organization.

10

FINAL THOUGHTS

Within any organization, you'll face many, many opinions about the best uses of employee surveys and their value to an organization. Some leaders (and employees for that matter) view surveys with great suspicion, not understanding how they can be used to help organizations become more productive or effective. They may believe that surveys do not accurately represent how employees think and feel about the company. They may tell you, "Only the unhappy employees respond to surveys" or, paradoxically, "Only happy employees take the survey." Neither is 100 percent true, of course. Employees may believe that their time participating in the survey is wasted, because leaders will pay attention to only the good news and ignore the bad.

In other organizations, the survey has become a revered process and source of data and insights, for better or for worse. It is possible for survey data to be overinterpreted, meaning that specific results that were originally intended to reflect employees' experience have been repurposed for performance evaluation or determining monetary bonuses for leaders and managers. Neither of these is a productive use of the data, and in my experience using survey data in this manner tips the balance of the survey process from an opportunity for employees to share what is going well and what isn't in the company to an exercise in ranking and rewarding managers, often accompanied by subtle pressure from the managers being ranked. Other companies love survey data almost too much, and try to quantify everything, grinding through analysis after analysis, but failing to feed the findings back to employees or take visible action to address issues.

Of course, many companies use the survey process to gain insight into the work experience and take the results very seriously. These companies develop question sets that reflect what is important to leaders and managers today and in the future, and they plan and implement actions driven by survey results at multiple levels of the organization. They return to the survey data set multiple times between data collections, mining the data to provide a continuous flow of information and guidance to the organization.

More often than not, all these situations occur within the same organization. In this case, an internal team may be responsible for creating a survey strategy that informs leaders about the effectiveness of the organization and provides ongoing insights that will help the company achieve its goals. Leaders and managers (and employees, to be truthful) may see the survey as a report card on engagement, a tool for ranking leaders, or even a process that should be viewed with suspicion, because the data aren't "real" and no one ever does anything with the results. How can we possibly shape the thinking of these groups so they all see the survey as a vibrant, insightful, conversation-starting and organization-improving tool?

If you are responsible for the survey process in your company and have high aspirations for how surveys can be used strategically in the organization, getting all parties on board with a reframing of the survey process may seem like an impossible task. There are simply too many constituent groups with too many opinions and too many past experiences with surveys. The reality is that transforming a survey process into a strategic tool that drives an engaging workplace won't happen overnight.

Instead, think of the survey as a marathon, one that attracts many runners from many places with different levels of experience. At the front of the pack are the elite runners who travel the world competing and will run the race at a record pace. Just behind them are competitive runners, although not quite at the elite level, who spend the bulk of their time training for just such races. Toward the end of the pack, and making up most of the runners, are the hobbyists, the weekend runners. These people have many approaches to preparing for the marathon and reasons for participating. Some want to beat their personal best, some just want to finish, and others are running to raise awareness of a specific cause. While they enjoy running, it is not the focus of their life, and they may only ever run one or two marathons.

The pack of runners in large marathons moves very slowly after the starting gun is fired, inching toward the starting line. Given the speed of the front runners, who leave the starting line first, and the pace with which the pack moves forward, the elite runners may be well on their way before the back of the pack reaches the starting line. The front-runners will complete the course before most of the pack is halfway through the course.

In that vein, change in an organization happens slowly, particularly in a large organization comprising hundreds or thousands of employees with highly diverse backgrounds, experiences, and expectations. Just as in the marathon analogy, a few forward thinkers who understand the possibilities of new ideas and processes lead the pack, and the rest follow behind at a variety of rates. Because it is impossible to get all employees and leaders across the finish line at the same time, it is important to adopt an evolutionary approach to shifting the organization's use of surveys. A company that is accustomed to using survey data to "rack and stack" managers will not immediately abandon that approach to focus on organization effectiveness and creating an engaging work environment. The thought leaders in the organization will need to create a plan to bring the rest of the organization along with them.

Old habits die hard, and that is especially true in organizations. Routines and ongoing processes encourage habits. These habits must evolve over time to accommodate new directions and strategies for the organization. Moving too quickly to establish new habits can create frustration and confusion for leaders and employees, which can result in a stubborn unwillingness to move to the new.

The most effective strategy is to maintain some of the old while introducing some of the new. Maintain some of the legacy survey focus and habits while introducing some of the features, topic areas, and analytics of the new approach. It is important to create a bridge from the legacy approach to surveys to the new, more strategic approach. Employees and leaders at the front of the pack will willingly come along with the new approach and quickly let go of the past, and those at the back can inch forward more slowly, with any reluctance toward a new approach assuaged by the comfort of retaining some legacy habits.

It is important to make good use of proof points during the transition process. Demonstrate the value of the new approach to surveys by providing insights and guidance in those areas that are top of mind for leaders. Providing timely insight on a key issue, helping them solve their problem, will encourage leaders to imagine what the new approach to surveys can yield. Create an experience, an aha moment, that helps leaders appreciate what survey data can do for the organization when the focus and administration of the process is reimagined to suit its strategic needs.

Throughout my years of practice, some of my most rewarding moments have come when a leader has said to me, "I never knew an employee survey could tell me that." They expected the same old table of numbers, but instead got insight into a critical organizational issue. A survey team that can consistently deliver that moment of clarity will quickly become a valued resource in the organization. With enough of these moments, providing managers and leaders with the insights they need to lead effectively, the pack starts moving more quickly toward the starting line.

Once the pack is moving, change can happen more quickly, and that helps the business. Successful organizations never stop evolving, which means that an organization's survey process cannot remain static and continue to meet its needs. The best and most effective survey processes continuously update the topics assessed; adopt new analyses, approaches, and technology; and find new ways to analyze results to stay current with the organization.

A survey is nothing more than a tool that collects data and information. It is not The Survey, a defined instrument and process. What does the organization need to know, and what does it need to do, to successfully achieve its goals? HR professionals who can answer that question and provide the data and insights leaders need will lead the pack to create an engaging workplace.

REFERENCES

Bersin, D. 2015. "Becoming Irresistible: A New Model for Employee Engagement." *Deloitte Review,* January 26. www2.deloitte.com/insights /us/en/deloitte-review/issue-16/employee-engagement-strategies.html.

Brown, D., V. Melian, M. Solow, S. Chheng, and K. Parker. 2015. *Culture and Engagement: The Naked Organization.* Deloitte, February 27. https:// dupress.deloitte.com/dup-us-en/focus/human-capital-trends/2015 /employee-engagement-culture-human-capital-trends-2015.html.

Celpax. 2017. "Measuring Employee Engagement." Celpax, July 29. www.celpax.com/measuring-employee-engagement.

Corporate Leadership Council. 2004. *Driving Performance and Retention Through Employee Engagement: A Quantitative Analysis of Effective Engagement Strategies.* Corporate Executive Board. http://cwfl.usc .edu/assets/pdf/Employee%20engagement.pdf.

Hofstede, G. 1984. *Culture's Consequences: International Differences in Work-Related Values,* 2nd ed. Beverly Hills, CA: SAGE Publications.

Johnson, S.R., and P.M. Mastrangelo. 2008. "Have You Ever Wondered If Survey 'Rules of Thumb' Are Valuable Tools for Data Interpretation?" Paper presented at the 23rd annual convention of the Society for Industrial/Organizational Psychology, San Francisco.

Kruse, K. 2012. "Employee Engagement Research (Master List of 32 Findings)." Kevin Kruse website, September 18. www.kevinkruse.com /employee-engagement-research-master-list-of-29-studies.

Masztal, J.J., D.M. Salamon, G. Pashturro, and L. Steelman. 2015. *Employees Can Make the Difference! Examining the Employee Survey Process in Fortune 500 and Mid-Sized Companies.* Burke. www.burke .com/Library/WhitePapers/BurkeEmployeeSurveyUse4p.pdf.

Ray, R.L., P. Hyland, D.A. Dye, J. Kaplan, and A. Pressman. 2014. *DNA of Engagement: How Organizations Create and Sustain Highly Engaging Cultures.* The Conference Board, October. www.conference -board.org/publications/publicationdetail.cfm?publicationid=2844.

Ulrich, D., et al. 2012. "Exclusive: The Six Competencies to Inspire HR Professionals for 2012." *HR* Magazine, January 4. www.hrmagazine .co.uk/article-details/exclusive-the-six-competencies-to-inspire-hr -professionals-for-2012.

ABOUT THE AUTHOR

Sarah Johnson is the vice president of enterprise surveys and analytics at Perceptyx, a leading survey consulting firm. Sarah has more than three decades of experience in her field. She specializes in employee engagement, organization development and effectiveness, and survey data analysis, advising senior leaders at Fortune 500 firms around the world.

Sarah has witnessed executives struggling across industries with such common challenges as guiding a global company through transformational change, leading successfully in turbulent times, and building employee engagement and retention among high-potential employees. Clients most often ask her how to leverage employee engagement to drive organization strategy. Her clients rely on her to capture the attention of senior leadership in a way that "makes the light bulb go on in their heads" when discussing employee engagement and alignment.

Sarah believes that companies need people who are not just book smart, but "maze bright"—people who can adapt to different cultures and continually changing circumstances, or as she puts it, who can "read the signs and figure out where to go from here." Organizational surveys can provide those signs, and Sarah is committed to helping leaders and managers develop their ability to analyze and use the data strategically.

Sarah works with clients around the world, from as far north as Denmark to as far south as Brazil. She received a bachelor's degree in psychology from Purdue University, and holds a master of arts degree and PhD in industrial/organizational psychology from the Ohio State University. Prior to joining Perceptyx, Sarah was the global survey practice leader at CEB, and a vice president at Genesee Services. Sarah has also worked as an internal consultant, leading the global organizational survey programs at Eastman Kodak and IBM. During her time at IBM, Sarah held a number of HR positions that gave her experience in employee relations, compensation, and resource planning. Sarah began her professional career at Procter & Gamble. She is the co-founder and first chairperson of the Information Technology Survey Group, a survey benchmarking and best practices organization for companies in the information technology industry, and was a member of the board of Mayflower Group survey benchmarking consortium.

A popular speaker, Sarah has made dozens of presentations at conferences sponsored by the Society for Industrial/Organizational Psychology (SIOP), Human Capital Institute, IQPC, HR.com, and many more. She has been a contributor to three books on surveys published by SIOP as part of its Frontier series.

INDEX

In this index, *f* denotes figure and *t* denotes table.

A

action planning
    about, 115–116
    capabilities, tailoring to managers', 121–124, 122*f*
    challenges, 35–36, 117–118
    as complicated, 118
    continuous listening and, 35–36
    custom survey content and, 123
    need for, 17–19
    nudges, building in, 124
    1-2-3 approach, 119–120, 120*f*
    simplifying, 118–119
    streamlining, 124
    survey result interpretation and, 110*f*, 111–112
administration of surveys, 31–33, 41–43, 123
adviser (HR role), 104*f*, 105

advocacy behavior, 3
analytics
    comment data, 87–88
    dust bowl empiricism, 81–82
    external contexts, weaving in, 85–87
    gut decisions *versus*, 78–79
    hypothesis-driven, 80–81
    importance of, 78–80
    industry, 96–97, 96*f*
    locale, 95–96, 96*f*
    organization level of employees, 97–100, 98*f*
    outcomes, linking with, 88–92, 90*t*
    patterns, common, 92–100
    pyramid, starting at top of, 83–85
    theory-driven, 82–83
    tips, 100–101
    years of service, 93–94, 94*f*
attrition, factors influencing, 89–92, 90*t*

B

behavioral elements of employee
  engagement, 3–4
benchmark data, 48–49, 57–58,
  86–87
Bersin, Josh, 63
business strategy of organization,
  28–29

C

capability builder (HR role), 107
capability of managers, 117,
  121–124, 122f
census surveys. *See also* continuous
  listening; pulse surveys
  advantages and disadvantages,
    39–40
  pulse surveys *versus*, 33,
    37–38, 39t
  strategic use of, 41–43
change
  introducing, 127–129
  in organization, 54–57
change champion (HR role), 107
coach (HR role), 104f, 105
comment data, 87–88, 111
commitment, acknowledging, 114
communication strategy, 21, 30
company
  business strategy of, 28–29
  employee intention to stay
    with, 3
  objective of, 25–26
  transformation of, 54–57
compensation and benefits, 63
Conference Board, 6
consultant (HR role), 104f,
  106–107, 113–114

continuous listening
  about, 33–36
  action planning and
    implementation, 35–36
  depth, 37–38
  focus, 37
  impact, 38
  owners, 37
  purpose, 36–37
conversation starter, surveys as,
  16–18
Corporate Leadership Council, 63
correlation coefficients, 65–66, 69t
credible activist (HR role), 106
cross-tabulation reports, 84
cultural challenges, 29
cultural differences, 57–58, 95–96,
  96f
custom survey content
  action planning and, 123
  benchmarking, external,
    48–49, 57–58
  business/culture
    transformation and,
    54–57
  constituent groups, 58–59, 60
  content, cohesive, 60
  creating, 57–60
  data, objective *versus*
    opinion, 53–54
  language, simple, 58
  message sent by, 54–57
  need for, 45–46
  past survey results, 57
  questions, additional, 60
  questions, core set of, 59
  report designs, 59
  response scale, 58
  senior leader interviews, 57

standardized survey content
    versus, 46–48
trend tracking *versus,* 49–53

D

daily pulse surveys, 34
data
    benchmark, 48–49, 57–58,
        86–87
    comment, 87–88, 111
    in hierarchy of impact, 108
    objective *versus* opinion,
        53–54
    owners of, 37
    reporting, 59, 84, 112
data analysis
    comments, 87–88
    dust bowl empiricism, 81–82
    external contexts, weaving in,
        85–87
    gut decisions *versus,* 78–79
    hypothesis-driven, 80–81
    importance of, 78–80
    industry, 96–97, 96f
    locale, 95–96, 96f
    organization level of
        employees, 97–100, 98f
    outcomes, linking with,
        88–92, 90t
    patterns, common, 92–100
    pyramid, starting at top of,
        83–85
    theory-driven, 82–83
    tips, 100–101
    years of service, 93–94, 94f
Deloitte, 63
demographic group differences, 111
differences between groups, 111

discretionary effort, 3
diversity and inclusion topics, 52,
    53
driver analysis, 64–68, 69t, 84
dust bowl empiricism, 81–82

E

Eastern Europe, 95, 96f
effectiveness, organization, 8–12,
    10f, 26–27, 69–74
employee engagement
    behavioral elements of, 3–4
    driving *versus* creating
        workplace conducive to,
        69–74
    early research on, 4–5
    evaluating, 24–25
    focus on, excessive, 5–8
    improving, plans for, 5–6
    organization effectiveness
        and, 8–12, 10f
    score, 5, 7–8, 61–62
    "what" of, 61–62
    "why" of, 62–64, 74–75
employee satisfaction, 2–3
employees, organization level of,
    97–100, 98f
engagement. *See* employee
    engagement
ethical compliance topics, 52, 53
experience and expertise, offering,
    113
external benchmarking, 48–49,
    57–58, 86–87

F

favorability scores, 111
flexible work arrangements, 63–64

focus
    continuous listening and, 37
    on employee engagement,
        5–8
    of surveys, 1, 2, 3, 12–14
frequency of surveys. *See* census
    surveys; continuous listening;
    pulse surveys

G

generalist (HR role), 104*f*, 105
groups, 58–59, 60, 111
gut decisions, 78–79

H

hierarchy of impact, 108–109,
    109*f*
history of organizational surveys,
    1–2
Hofstede, Geert, 95
honeymoon effect, 93, 95*f*
"How was your day?" buttons, 34
HR innovator and integrator (HR
    role), 106–107
human resources (HR)
    challenges, 28
    organizational success,
        contribution to, 26
    role continuum, 104–107,
        104*f*
    survey results, use of,
        107–109, 109*f*
hypothesis-driven analytics, 80–81
impact
    of continuous listening, 38
    hierarchy of, 108–109, 109*f*
    refining, 110*f*, 111–112
industry patterns, 97–98, 96*f*

influencers, 84
information, in hierarchy of
    impact, 109
insight, in hierarchy of impact,
    109
intention to stay with company, 3

J

Japan, 95–96, 96*f*
job satisfaction, 2–3

K

Kruse, Kevin, 4

L

language, simple, 58
Latin America, 95, 96*f*
leaders, senior
    custom survey content,
        creating, 57
    interviewing, 29, 57
    result patterns, common,
        97–99, 98*f*
    survey strategy, including in,
        27, 29
listening, continuous
    about, 33–36
    action planning and
        implementation, 35–36
    depth, 37–38
    focus, 37
    impact, 38
    owners, 37
    purpose, 36–37
locale, 95–96, 96*f*

M

managers, capability of, 117, 121–124, 122*f*

marathon analogy, 127–128

marketplace challenges, 28

N

negative results, 20–21

nudges, building in, 124

O

objective data, 53–54

objective of organization, 25–26

1-2-3 approach to action planning, 119–120, 120*f*

ongoing effort, surveys as, 19–20

opinion data from employees, 53–54

opinions about surveys, 125–126

organization

    business strategy of, 28–29

    employee intention to stay with, 3

    objective of, 25–26

    transformation of, 54–57

organization effectiveness, 8–12, 10*f*, 26–27, 69–74

organization level of employees, 97–100, 98*f*

organization performance, 2–3, 9, 10*f*

organization satisfaction, 2–3

organizational group differences, 111

organizational success, 8–12, 10*f*, 26–27, 69–74

organizational surveys. *See* surveys; *specific topics*

outcomes, linking survey results with, 88–92, 90*t*

owners, data, 37

P

participation rates, 37–38, 111

perceptions, 113

performance, organization, 2–3, 9, 10*f*

positive divergence analysis, 68, 69*t*

proof points, 119, 128–129

pulse surveys. *See also* census surveys; continuous listening

    advantages and disadvantages, 40–41

    census surveys *versus*, 33, 37–38, 39*t*

    daily, 34

    strategic use of, 41–43

Q

questions

    additional, 60

    core set of, 59

    of the day, 34

R

random analysis, 81–82

reasons for conducting surveys, 24–26

reframing survey process, 127–129

relative weights analysis, 66–67, 69*t*

reporting data, 59, 84, 112 –113

response rate, 37–38, 111

response scale, 58

results, survey

action planning and, 110f, 111–112
comments, 111
favorability scores, 111
groups, differences between, 111
hierarchy of impact, 108–109, 109f
HR use of, 107–109, 109f
impact, refining, 110f, 111–112
interpreting, 109–112, 110f
negative, 20–21
outcomes, linking with, 88–92, 90t
past, 57
reporting data, 112–113
reviewing, 110f, 111
themes, defining, 110f, 111
role expectations, 20

S

scores
employee engagement, 5, 7–8, 61–62
favorability, 111
senior leaders
custom survey content, creating, 57
interviewing, 29, 57
result patterns, common, 97–99, 98f
survey strategy, including in, 27, 29
service, years of employee, 93–94, 94f

standardized survey content, 46–48. See also custom survey content
strategic positioner (HR role), 107
strategy. See also survey strategy
business, 28–29
communication, 21, 30
structural equation modeling, 67–68, 69t
success, organizational, 8–12, 10f, 26–27, 69–74
survey administration, 31–33, 41–43, 123
survey content. See custom survey content
survey frequency. See census surveys; continuous listening; pulse surveys
survey results
action planning and, 110f, 111–112
comments, 111
favorability scores, 111
groups, differences between, 111
hierarchy of impact, 108–109, 109f
HR use of, 107–109, 109f
impact, refining, 110f, 111–112
interpreting, 109–112, 110f
negative, 20–21
outcomes, linking with, 88–92, 90t
past, 57
reporting data, 112–113
reviewing, 110f, 111
themes, defining, 110f, 111

survey strategy
    about, 19–20, 23–24
    developing, 28–30
    organizational success,
        contribution to, 26–27
    reasons for conducting
        survey, 24–26
    surveys as means to end,
        19–20
surveys. *See also specific topics*
    administration of, 31–33,
        41–43, 123
    advantages of, 15–16
    as conversation starter, 16–18
    focus of, 1, 2, 3, 12–14
    history of organizational, 1–2
    as means to end, 18–21
    as ongoing effort, 19–20
    opinions about, 125–126
    reasons for conducting,
        24–26

T

tactician (HR role), 104–105, 104f
technology, in survey
    administration, 31–33
technology proponent (HR role),
    107
themes, defining, 110f, 111
theory-driven analytics, 82–83
trends, tracking, 49–53

U

Ulrich, Dave, 106–107
union vulnerability indicator, 82
United States, 95, 96f

W

Western Europe, 95, 96f
"what" of employee engagement,
    61–62
"why" of employee engagement,
    62–64, 74–75
workplace conducive to employee
    engagement, 69–74

Y

years of service, employee, 93–94,
    94f